My Mother Only Had Me for the Check

CLARICE JEFFERIES
PUBLISHING

My Mother Only Had Me for the Check

by

Crystal Bass

Edited by

Sofia Artola Diaz

Published by

Clarice Jefferies Publishing

Contact info: cjpublishing@yahoo.com

Disclaimer

The stories in this book reflect my recollection of events. Apart from my husband and psychologists, names of individuals have been changed and or modified to protect the privacy of those depicted. Dialogue has been re-created from memory.

TABLE OF CONTENTS

MY DEAREST DAUGHTERS

As I sit down to share these words with you, my heart fills with a blend of pride, love, and a touch of bittersweet reflection. There are things I wish I had known, lessons I wish I could've imparted differently, and moments I wish I could rewind to amend any hurt I might have unintentionally caused you both.

Life is a peculiar journey. We navigate through it armed with the information and the wisdom passed down by our parents. But sometimes, that trove of knowledge is less vast than we'd hope. Occasionally, we learn as we go, figuring things out on the fly and bumping our heads along the way.

I realized decades ago that my "parental toolkit," my collection of lessons and understanding, was filled with many gaps. There were moments when my decisions might not have aligned with your expectations or even caused you pain. For that, I genuinely apologize.

You see, life isn't just about our choices; it's also about the information we possess to make those choices. Sometimes, we're navigating without a map, without a manual. I might not have had the financial stability I wished for, the resources I dreamed of providing, or the unwavering support from your fathers. But that lack didn't dilute the boundless love I've always held for you both.

You've grown into remarkable women, and every step you've taken has filled me with an awe I cannot articulate. Your strength and resilience are testaments to your spirits and the love and values we shared through those imperfect moments.

Life isn't about being flawless; it's about embracing and learning from our imperfections. It's about recognizing that sometimes; our best is simply the best we can muster with the cards we've been dealt.

Despite any shortcomings, I've remained fiercely proud of the remarkable individuals you've become. You've blossomed beautifully, each petal a testament to your strength and determination. Know this: my love for you remains unwavering and steadfast in the face of any falsehoods, mistakes, or missteps. You've inherited my love for you and the wisdom that comes from acknowledging our imperfections and growing more robust because of them.

As I move forward, I'll be here—always, unequivocally—ready to support, love, and cherish you, just as I have from the very start.

With all my love

PREFACE

As a woman, I was conditioned to think that outward beauty is everything.

After the birth of my second child, I became relentless about my appearance. I vowed to always wear make-up, even if I were going to stay at home. I made a pact with myself to consistently look put-together. And while I've always taken pride in my looks, I've come to realize, with the passage of time, I was using my appearance to mask my pain.

I struggled with depression and anxiety. I wrestled with anger, forgiveness, and trust. I did not know how to love myself and often felt like I was wearing my emotions on my sleeve. I wanted to hide my pain from the world, but I didn't know how...that's when I discovered cosmetics.

Every morning, I put on my make-up and styled my hair, hoping the beauty I projected on the outside would distract me from the pain I felt inside. With a little foundation, concealer, blush, and mascara, I could transform my face and cover up the bags under my eyes from lack of sleep. I could erase the redness from crying and the blemishes from stress. I could present a calm, composed image to the world, even when I was falling apart inside.

Behind my carefully curated image was a woman struggling with deep emotional pain. I had been raped and beaten by my uncle and repeatedly molested and beaten by my mother's boyfriend. I experienced trauma in a way that was unfair and robbed me of my innocence and childhood. I didn't know how to deal with the pain, and instead of facing it head-on, I buried it deep inside me.

For a while, it worked. People would complement me on my looks, and I would feel a fleeting sense of happiness, but I was only masking my pain, not dealing with it. And as much as I tried to ignore it, my pain would always resurface, often in unexpected and complicated ways.

I became an excellent make-up artist. I was meticulous with my brushes and pencils. I had the unique ability to take multiple colors, splash them across my face, and create something beautiful. Often, men who came across my artwork would tell me how beautiful I was, unaware of what laid behind my daily creations, unaware of the mental torment driving each brush stroke. Unaware of the suicide attempt hidden behind the bold lines of my pencils.

I've been wearing make-up every day since my early 20s. Now, I'm 59, and I realize I've spent multiple decades splashing the same colors across a face that seemed familiar to me, yet I was unfamiliar with who I was looking at. Day after day, month after month, and year after year, I had been looking at the reflection of a woman that I recognized...but did not know.

MY MOTHER

My childhood home was one of many in our neighborhood. It was a place where chaos reigned, the concept of bedtime was laughable, and partying was the norm. My mother was what you might call a "party mom," thriving on late nights, strange company, and an endless supply of alcohol and drugs. She was the ringleader of our family's perpetual carnival.

My earliest memories are hazy, filled with laughter, music, and a constant buzz of activity. While other kids were in bed by 8 p.m., my nights were filled with the arrivals and departures of customers whose names I wouldn't know. In our house, there were always strange men and women, their faces a blur of eccentricity. But one woman stood out: I will call her Lisa, my mother's closest friend.

Lisa was like my mother's sister. They had been friends for as long as I could remember, and their bond was unbreakable.

Parties would reach new heights when they were together. They were the dynamic duo, the life of our house's never-ending parties.

As I grew older, I realized Lisa was the driving force behind many of these wild nights. It wasn't just her charismatic personality but the sense of adventure and freedom she brought with her that my mother craved. They were unstoppable, a whirlwind of partying and excess that knew no bounds.

Then, one day, my mother made an unusual request. It had been a particularly wild weekend, and the house was still littered with empty bottles and other relics of overabundance. With a gleam in her eye, my mother turned to Lisa and said, "You should move in with us," with a sincerity I hadn't heard before.

Lisa, usually quick with a witty retort, paused. She looked around at the chaos of our house, then at me and my two younger siblings, who were playing on the kitchen floor with empty liquor bottles amongst the disorder.

"Why would I do something like that?" Lisa finally inquired; her voice tinged with apprehension.

My mother's reaction was immediate, as if she had been anticipating this moment for years.

"Why not? We can throw parties whenever we want. We'd be living the dream, just you and me."

Lisa's laughter filled the room, but it was a different kind of laughter, a laughter that carried an unsettling truth with it.

She leaned close to my mother and spoke softly, as if trying to keep her words away from me and my siblings.

"Look, I love partying with you, but you have three kids to look after. You can't just abandon them. It isn't right."

My mother's face changed from excitement to disappointment; her dreams of an endless party house shattered like glass. The silence that followed was deafening, only broken by the distant sounds of children's laughter out in the street, a stark reminder of the life we were missing out on.

All it took was that fateful conversation, for Lisa to turn down my mother's invitation to live with us permanently. My mother was hurt by the rejection, and instead of dealing with her disappointment like a responsible adult, she reacted in the most perplexing way possible. Her eyes were filled with resentment and frustration as she faced me and my two younger siblings.

"From now on," she declared, her voice trembling with a strange resolve, "don't call me mom anymore... you call me Ms. Lady."

Lisa was never asked to move in again after that day. Instead, our house remained a revolving door of strange faces and wild nights, a place where my siblings and I learned to navigate a dangerous and mysterious world. But I could tell my mother yearned for the days when she and Lisa were the queens of their own never-ending party, before the reality of motherhood ruined her fun.

MS. LADY

Ms. Lady was the mother of three children: two girls and a boy. The eldest of the trio was me, Crystal. My younger brother and I share a three-year age gap, while my sister, the youngest among us, came into the world four years after my birth. Tragically, my sister is no longer with us, as she fell victim to a heinous crime in the late 1990s.

Strangely, Ms. Lady harbored an intense aversion toward me, and I couldn't help but believe that it stemmed from my resemblance to my father, Bill. My father had been Ms. Lady's first love, a fact I learned through my maternal grandmother. Ms. Lady gave birth to me when she was 17 years old. At that time, Ms. Lady and my father, were neighbors in the same apartment complex and attended the same high school.

Bill's mother had caught wind of a rumor circulating about Ms. Lady being pregnant, which piqued her curiosity. She decided to act by arranging a meeting with my grandmother, Ms. Lady, and my father. They embarked on a trip to the hospital to confirm the veracity of the gossip. Once the doctor confirmed Ms. Lady's pregnancy, Bill's mother drove the group home. She dropped off Ms. Lady and my grandmother, and a few days later, she packed up my father's belongings and they left Fresno, California, never to return.

So, my father left us long before I was born, leaving Ms. Lady to carry the emotional weight of his absence. As a child, I couldn't fully grasp the intricacies of adult relationships, but I could keenly sense the void that his departure had created. Little did I anticipate that Ms. Lady's bitterness toward him would ultimately find an unexpected target: me.

I was just a child longing for Ms. Lady's love, attention, and approval, but instead, I became the recipient of her pent-up frustration and anger. The love she had for my absent father tainted the love she should have had for nurturing and protecting me. Her rage toward him seeped into our interactions, gradually eroding my self-esteem and sense of worth.

Her love was conditional, and I constantly tried to prove my worth to receive even a sliver of her attention. Every mistake I made was magnified, and every small accomplishment was overshadowed by what she saw as my father's failures. I craved the love and attention of a mother who should have been my rock, my guiding light through life's ups and downs.

Instead, I became lost in the shadows of her twisted priorities. Her friends, and endless parties took precedence over my well-being and happiness.

Her judgment, clouded by drugs and alcohol, took her away from reality and numbed her emotions. I wished she could have been present to see the pain in my

eyes and the loneliness in my heart, but she was stuck in a cycle that seemed impossible to break. Friends became constant companions for Ms. Lady, and she traded meaningful connections for fleeting encounters. The love she put into those parties rang through our house, but the love never included me.

As the days and weeks turned into months and years, I was forced to become self-sufficient and independent. I took on experiences no child should ever experience. It was a heavy burden to bear, leaving scars on my body that would forever remind me of the childhood I never had.

CLEANING FOR LOVE

Growing up, Ms. Lady became more of a phantom figure than a nurturing presence. My childhood was far from the storybooks – no bedtime tales, no warm hugs, and definitely no schoolyard picnics.

I never had the comforting embrace of a mother's love or the security of a stable home as a child. Instead, I found myself navigating a maze of uncertainty, never truly knowing where I belonged.

Her absence created a void that no one else could fill. I yearned for her love, guidance, and nurturing touch, but she always seemed preoccupied with other problems, unable to accept responsibility for raising me. My heart ached as I saw other children embrace their mothers, and I yearned for the same connection.

Although living with various family friends put a roof over my head, it never felt like home. Each new location brought new faces, new rules, new abuses, and new dynamics to learn. It was like trying to combine puzzle pieces but never finding the perfect fit and while some people I lived with were familiar, there was always an underlying sense of impermanence. I couldn't shake the feeling that I was just a temporary guest and that, at any moment, I might be shuffled off to yet another unfamiliar place.

My education was never a top concern for Ms. Lady. When she couldn't secure a stable place for me to live, she made a unique choice. Instead of enrolling me in elementary school like most children, she sent me to Santa Barbara, California, to reside with my grandfather. He had a stern demeanor, but he was there - a presence that was sorely lacking in my relationship with Ms. Lady. I was a child, barely old enough to tie my shoelaces, but I found myself immersed in the daily grind of cleaning apartment complexes as part of my grandfather's business.

I could see other kids my age skipping down the streets, their laughter echoing through the air, but for me, fun was a fleeting notion, an elusive dream I could only grasp in my imagination. My grandfather was kind in his own way but focused on making ends meet, leaving little room for affection or attention. While the experience taught me valuable lessons, it's impossible to ignore the fact that I was unknowingly caught in the web of forced child labor.

While other children were learning to read and write, I worked. Trying to make sense of a world that seemed indifferent to my existence. It was tough, but I had to grow up fast. There were no play-dates or sleepovers; my days were consumed with intensive labor, cleaning dozens of apartment units and making them shine like new. From washing walls, doors and windows, to scrubbing dirty floors, sinks, and toilets.

This work was grueling, and as the hours passed, exhaustion set in, and my tiny body ached from the physical strain. But I pushed through, confused by a sense of obligation and a desire to be loved and wanted by a family member.

As time went by, I began to resent Ms. Lady more and more. Why had she abandoned me like this? What did I do to deserve such neglect? I yearned for her to swoop in, apologize, and take me back. But the months passed, and her absence persisted, like a shadow lurking in the corners of my heart.

School became a distant concept, a missed opportunity. As a child, I didn't understand that education was crucial for a better life; all I knew was that I didn't have the chance to pursue it. My dreams of learning to read and write faded away, replaced by the harsh reality of surviving day to day.

MS. LADY TO THE RESCUE

After returning from Santa Barbara, I attended elementary school sporadically. During those times, Ms. Lady was never the type to participate in parent-teacher conferences or PTA meetings. It was as if these gatherings existed in another universe, one she didn't find necessary to consider. On days where I would stay after school, I remember seeing my classmates' mothers walking onto the school campus, greeting teachers, and forming connections beyond the classroom. Meanwhile, Ms. Lady's disinterest left me with an unbearable mix of longing and resentment.

Then, there was that one occasion when my world spun on its axis. Like any other afternoon in my elementary school classroom, the hum of childish chatter filled the air. I sat with my friends, our laughter rippling through the room like a river of happiness. I allowed myself a moment of thoughtlessness among the laughter and joined in the shenanigans. The laughter was directed at one of Ms. Lady's friends who worked at my school as a teacher's aide. However, I was unaware that she had singled out my laughter amongst the crowded classroom.

A few hours later, as I was struggling with a reading assignment, I unexpectedly looked up, and there stood Ms. Lady, her face a mixture of rage and dissatisfaction. As the room went from cheerful chatter to stunned silence, time seemed to stand still. My classmates' eyes widened, capturing a scene of humiliation and vulnerability that would stay with me forever.

Ms. Lady stood there, holding a belt, a visual reminder of my impending humiliation. The teacher's eyes, which had once been filled with warmth and encouragement, now held an uneasy mixture of sympathy and shock. I was paralyzed like a deer caught in headlights.

"Come here!" She shouted as she pointed to the floor in front of her. As I walked toward the front of my classroom, she shouted, "Get down on your hands and knees!"

I bit my lower lip to keep the tears at bay as the belt landed with a sting.

Ms. Lady's vulgar tirade of profanity echoed throughout the room, each sentence a stark reminder of my careless actions. I wanted nothing more than to vanish, to escape the sea of young eyes fixed on me, eyes filled with pity, confusion, and possibly trauma.

The belt hurt physically, but the humiliation damaged me even more. It was as if a spotlight had been shone on my flaws, highlighting them for all to see. My cheeks burned with shame as I struggled with the opposing emotions of rage at Ms. Lady and frustration with myself.

That memory has never completely faded in the years since. It reminds me of the complexities of human emotions and actions and how they intersect unexpectedly. It's a chapter I go back to, not to wallow in self-pity but to accept the pain and embarrassment as part of my journey, a chapter that shaped me and fueled my hatred for Ms. Lady. Her unexpected appearance in the classroom, though unusual and deeply unsettling, spoke volumes about her determination to convey a lesson—a lesson that extended far beyond academic subjects.

THE BOOSTER

Growing up in the vibrant, often enigmatic streets of the 1970s and 80s, my world was an intricate blend of innocence and intrigue. During those early years, I witnessed the fascinating development of the relationships that Ms. Lady held with whom she called her friends. Relationships that involved a subtle dance of secrets and concealed activities.

Ms. Lady always welcomed the neighborhood criminals with a genuine and comforting warmth. But beneath her friendly smile was an undercurrent of mystery that I couldn't quite grasp. I could only begin to get a glimpse of what lay beneath the surface through the hushed conversations and whispered discussions.

The term "boosting" reverberated through the walls of our home, evoking feelings of adventure and camaraderie. As a child, I had a talent for piecing together fragments of adult conversations, often resulting in an incomplete and distorted combination of understanding. Boosting, as I understood it, was a magical act in which clothes traded hands and found new homes. I had yet to learn that this attraction had a darker origin, involving a shadowy world of theft, deception, and crime.

Boosting was a shared endeavor in Ms. Lady's circle of friends, a bond that transcended societal norms. With their eclectic personalities and contagious laughter, these women would gather around tables overflowing with clothes, casually discussing their latest finds and trades over alcohol and marijuana.

Unbeknownst to my young mind, these seemingly innocent chats masked a scheme that went beyond the bounds of legality. I stood there in awe as they reveled in their newfound riches, never doubting the legitimacy of their accomplishments.

But of all the visitors passing through our home, my favorite was my Uncle T, one of Ms. Lady's younger brothers, whose swagger held an air of mystery that sparked my interest. His visits were infrequent, but they always created a sense of anticipation. He'd show up with bags stuffed to the gills, each containing a treasure trove of clothing and jewelry that would soon end up in the hands of the boosting circle. I admired his sense of pride, his confidence, a beacon that drew me closer to comprehending the mystery unfolding before me.

Curiosity eventually gave way to awareness, and the puzzle pieces began to fall into place. The shroud of innocence that had cloaked my perception began to lift, revealing a troubling and fascinating reality. I learned that the term "boosting" was a euphemism for theft, not just a playful synonym for acquiring fashionable attire. The clothes that changed hands and the laughter that filled the air were all part of a larger story in which the stolen goods were the main attraction.

As my understanding grew, so did my participation in this intricate dance. My thirst for love and attention was, for some reason, still at an all-time high, and the rush to be a part of something so daring and rebellious was irresistible. It became simple to slip into the role.

My group of friends was a mishmash of personalities, each with our own quirks and dreams. We were drawn together not only by proximity but also by an unspoken understanding that went beyond words. We had a code of conduct among us, an unbreakable pact formed around the idea of boosting—our ticket to a world where friendship and adventure intertwined.

Our adventures began innocently enough, fueled by a combination of curiosity and the thrill of secrecy. The idea of trading goods amongst us initially appeared innocent, like a child's version of economic exchange.

Candy bars snatched from convenience stores; colorful trinkets tucked into pockets—these were our world's currencies. Our secret conversations were met with grins in a grand, shared endeavor that only we could comprehend.

It was only a matter of time before our ambitions grew beyond the realm of sugary valuables. Our quick fingers and quick wits progressed from candy bars to coveted clothing items obtained through a combination of stealth and daring. It was as if each heist brought us closer together, tying us in a bond that went beyond the thrill of acquisition. The clothes we "boosted" became symbols of our solidarity, our own secret society of friendship.

Our confidence expanded with each successful operation, as did our shared moral compass. We were confronted with questions we hadn't anticipated: was it wrong, and where did our limits lie? Our young minds wrestled with the gray areas of our actions, testing the limits of our developing personalities. As we faced the conflict between our desires and the weight of conventional wisdom, our bond grew more pungent, cementing our link as confidantes navigating uncertain terrain.

My actions were motivated by more than a desire to claim forbidden spoils; they manifested my need to belong. In the company of my friends, I felt a genuine and fulfilling sense of togetherness. We laughed, shared secrets, and celebrated our victories. Our friendship turned into an anchor that provided comfort and understanding in a world that was often abusive and lonely.

Our paths veered as we got older, with each of us embarking on our own unique journeys. However, my memories remained etched in my mind, a testament to a time when boosting was more than just a word—it was my symbol of bravery and the friendships I formed in the fiery atmosphere of my home life.

Ms. Lady's Arrest

I was standing outside our apartment, watching my younger brother and sister playing in the front yard, when a familiar sight caught my eye. A police car with flashing red and blue lights stood at the entrance to the neighborhood.

A police officer used the PA system to ask if anyone could identify the woman in the backseat. I looked at the rear of the patrol car, and my heart initially

skipped a beat; the shadows from the tree branches obscured the woman's face, but

it was unmistakably her, Ms. Lady.

I was torn for a moment while my younger sister began to cry, and my younger brother stood in shock, my mind raced with thoughts of Ms. Lady's unwillingness to love me. I still craved her love and affection; however, it never came. Instead, I received nothing but abuse and neglect.

A part of me knew I should go to her and offer her support or, at the very least, go to the officers and acknowledge her presence. However, the other part of me resisted. The pain of a mom who had beat me in front of my classmates left an imprint, and forgiveness was challenging.

Ms. Lady and I locked eyes as the police car drove away. It was only a moment, but it felt like time had stopped. In those few seconds, we exchanged a slew of emotions: sorrow, regret, anger, and an unspoken longing for a connection that seemed irreparable. My decision not to acknowledge her weighed heavily on my heart, but I couldn't deny the pain and anger within me.

As night fell, I couldn't get my mind off Ms. Lady in the police car. I wondered what she could have done that landed her in that backseat. But, more than that, I wrestled with my decision to distance myself from her.

I wondered if I'd made the right choice by not speaking up, by letting her be taken away without saying anything. Perhaps my silence increased the distance between us, leaving her to bear the consequences alone. But perhaps more than that... I struggled with not feeling guilty at all.

It's unclear what crime she committed that landed her in the back of that police car, but it wouldn't be her only run-in with the law. Ms. Lady would later serve time in a women's correctional facility. She and her long-term boyfriend, Ernest, were named as suspects in the armed robbery of an elderly couple.

I only attended one of her trials; Ms. Lady was eventually convicted as an accomplice to the crime. She hugged me before serving her sentence; it was the only time she showed me any affection, and for years, I felt guilty for not feeling bad about her circumstances.

UNCLE P

My Uncle P was Ms. Lady's youngest brother. When Ms. Lady was at work, my uncle would come over and watch me and my younger brother and sister. Those times were like a treasure chest full of joy, laughter, and fun.

During the times he watched us, my younger brother, sister, and Uncle would go into the laundry room, armed with a shared sense of excitement. Our mission was straightforward: gather up the dirty clothes and create the largest possible pile.

Our laughter grew louder as the pile grew taller. We couldn't wait to jump in. Leaping into that heap was pure joy—a moment of complete freedom and unbridled happiness. We'd roll around, burying ourselves beneath the sea of towels and clothes, as if we were in our own problem-free world. It was in that pile of clothes where my uncle would begin to touch me.

I had no one to teach me about "good touch, bad touch," no one to guide me or to talk with about what was taking place. I thought it was just how kids and adults played. I thought it was how families expressed love for one another.

My Uncle's eyes twinkled with delight as he joined in on our antics. He'd lift and swing me around, filling my heart with love. He was more than an uncle in those precious moments; he was a playmate, a confidant, and a guiding light that illuminated the wonders of childhood.

I remember the day my trust and love were betrayed—a moment that forever altered the dynamics of our relationship and my life. It was the day my uncle raped me.

I was at my grandmother's house. My younger sister and brother played outside in the backyard, and my grandmother was at work. My uncle was there, and two of his girlfriends from high school were visiting. All three of them were in the living room, having a good time talking, joking, and laughing.

Then something happened, and the girls got up and began to leave. I remember my uncle trying to talk fast to get them to stay, but the girls eventually made their way to the front door and walked out. I remember the look on his face, he was angry, but I didn't understand why. When the girls left, I decided to go outside into the backyard and play with my brother and sister. I got up to walk out, and that is when he grabbed me by the arm.

He grabbed me so hard that it scared me. I tried to pull away, but he had a firm grasp on me, and he began to pull me down the hallway toward my grandmother's bedroom. I was trying to grasp everything that I could to pull myself away. I remember grabbing my grandmother's clothes hanging from her bedroom door, but I could not hold onto them.

I fell to the floor and grabbed the door jamb to avoid being pulled into the bedroom. I began screaming for help, but my younger brother and sister could not hear me. He picked me up from the floor and threw me onto his mother's bed. I was kicking and screaming, trying desperately to keep my pants on. I remember scratching his face with my fingernails; he punched me in the stomach and slapped me across the face. I reached up to cover my face to shield myself, and that's when he pulled my pants and panties completely off.

The hysterical look on my uncle's face is forever branded into my memory. It's as if he did not see me; he was staring at me, and I was staring into his eyes, hoping he would realize what he was doing. I hoped he would see me and remember my love for him...but the strangest thing happened... I don't remember physically getting up, and I don't recall physically leaving the room, but I remember hearing myself screaming as I walked away.

I don't know how much time passed while I was lying there, but I remember being thrown back into my body and somehow being able to kick and shout, "I'm going to tell on you!" I remember my uncle saying sarcastically, "No one is going to believe you. Ms. Lady doesn't even care about you."

The betrayal felt sickening; my heart, along with my body, had been ripped apart. I was filled with various emotions, including rage, sadness, and disbelief. How could someone I loved and trusted violate me in the most despicable way? Why did he choose to hurt me so profoundly? These questions plagued my thoughts, leaving me with more questions than answers.

When we returned home, I told Ms. Lady what my uncle had done to me. She stood silent, listening to my story. When I was done speaking, she stared at me for a few seconds, then turned around and walked away. Weeks after that heartbreaking experience, I distanced myself from her and the rest of my family, erecting barriers around my heart to protect myself from further pain.

I often struggle with feeling like I am still that little girl trying to get out of that room. Looking back on my childhood, I often feel like the price I have had to pay for being Ms. Lady's daughter was too high... I hope the welfare check she had me for was worth every penny.

RICHARD

One day, I came across a Richard Pryor comedy album while flipping through Ms. Lady's record collection. The bold letters of his name caught my eye for some reason, and a spark of inspiration ignited within me. What if I could use this album cover to teach myself how to spell my last name?

With determination in my heart, I began studying the letters and memorizing them. I traced my fingers over the curves and lines, mentally repeating the sequence. It became a daily ritual, a reminder that learning can take unexpected forms.

I gradually began to recognize the letters of my last name outside of the context of the album cover. It was as if the album cover had become a key to a world of letters and words that had previously eluded me. I felt a sense of accomplishment I had never felt before.

My spelling did not improve, but I could remember the shapes of the letters and the order in which they were placed; it wasn't soon after that I could add the remaining letters at the end to spell my last name.

Ms. Lady met Richard when I was in sixth grade. I recall taking the bus home from elementary school. We lived in West Fresno, The Westgates apartment complex was where we lived at the time.

I don't remember when the beatings started, but I remember the pain. It was excruciating. Richard was a big man, over 6ft tall and well over 200 pounds. When he hit you once, it felt like your skin was falling off.

Like many other children, I would play along the sidewalk on the way home. Richard would be home when I arrived from school, and if I were one minute late, I would get a beating. Many times, due to the distance of the walk, I would come home late, and for my punishment, Richard would make me remove my clothes and bend over. I can remember feeling very uncomfortable. I felt like he would use the beating as an excuse to get me out of my clothes so that he could look at me naked. Shortly after, Richard began sneaking into my bedroom and sticking his hands down my pajamas as I slept. I would wake up from a deep sleep with my vagina in pain and see Richard leaving my bedroom.

I remember the day I found the courage to tell Ms. Lady that Richard was touching me, but instead of finding protection, I was again met with disbelief and inaction. My plea went unheard, and my pain was magnified as she ignored the truth. The man who should have been held accountable for his despicable actions was shielded by the person who should have been my defender.

In a moment of weakness, I made the fatal mistake of confiding in the person who was allowing my pain. Richard interpreted my words as a threat to his freedom, so my innocence was met with malice. He unleashed his rage on me in cruel retaliation, grabbing my head and slamming it onto the kitchen table. As I sat there, held down by Richard's monstrous grip, Ms. Lady told me she never wanted to hear me say anything like that again.

Once again, I was left to fend for myself. I ran to my room and slammed my door. My bedroom was my sanctuary, where I sought peace and calmness. Yet, I couldn't escape the inevitable. I would have to prepare myself for the looming darkness.

Evenings was when Ms. Lady would depart for her night shift, leaving me at the mercy of Richard.

The fear of what would happen next consumed me. I had to protect myself, so I barricaded the door with my heavy dresser, hoping it would deter him from entering my room.

With trembling hands, I pushed the massive piece of furniture, driven by a mix of terror and desperation. The harsh sound of wood scraping against the carpet was a reminder of the torment that lay ahead. It was also the sound of a young girl holding onto her last shreds of hope.

I slid to the floor once the blockade was in place, my back against the cool surface of the dresser. I hugged my knees to my chest for comfort. Tears would well up, silently tracing their paths down my cheeks, carrying away the anguish I couldn't bring myself to express.

I clung to memories of a simpler time, cleaning apartments in Santa Barbara, a time when the weight of the world had not yet crushed my innocence. Those memories were my lifeline, an anchor in the storm, reminding me that somewhere deep within, a glimmer of the girl I hoped to be remained.

MY AUNTIE VS RICHARD

Ms. Lady's choices of men were deplorable; Richard proves this theory, and it seemed like abuse followed me like a shadow. But amid the chaos, there was someone who became a temporary beacon of protection, my Auntie.

My Auntie had a fierce yet nurturing spirit. So, when it became clear that Richard was a threat, she stepped in to shield me from harm.

It all started when Richard, whose presence had always gloomed over our home, insisted that the old, rickety swing set in our backyard be removed before winter arrived. It might have been a reasonable request, but the way he made it sent shivers down my spine. He insisted on us dismantling it, even though it was an activity better suited for an adult.

My little brother was doing his best to be helpful, but his pace was too slow for Richard. Richard's eyes were red with rage as he barked orders at him. Frustrated with my brothers' slow pace, Richard did the unthinkable, he picked him up and slammed him onto the grass. My heart was racing, and my stomach was churning with rage and fear as my little brother lay motionless.

Without a second thought, I dashed inside to find Ms. Lady, hoping she would help. Unbeknownst to me, my Auntie was visiting that day. She'd always been a firecracker, and her presence in our home would soon be the catalyst for an unforgettable chain of events.

I burst into the house, gasping for breath and yelling out the injustice I had just witnessed. Ms. Lady listened without concern and without surprise on her face. In my moment of vulnerability, once again, Ms. Lady failed to respond. She seemed paralyzed, unable or unwilling to intervene.

"And where the hell did you go?" Richard's booming voice echoed through the yard as I returned outside to check on my brother.

I didn't hold back. "I went to tell Ms. Lady on you," I declared confidently. My rage and love for my younger brother and sister were unrestrained.

Richard's face twisted with fury; a sight I'd grown accustomed to. He directed his rage at me without hesitation. He grabbed me by the neck, choked me, and hurled me into our wooden fence, face-first. My eyelid was sliced open, and I could feel the sting of blood trickling into my eye.

I was lying on the ground, my world spinning around me, when I noticed my auntie approaching Richard with a shotgun. Panic overcame me as I realized she had taken it from the mantle in our living room.

My auntie, a woman of few words but ferocious action, didn't waste any time. As Richard slowly turned to face her, she racked the shotgun; the sound echoed through the yard like a thunderclap. As I lay there in awe and fear, time seemed to stand still.

The swing set in our backyard had no meaning at that point. It had been replaced by an intense clash between my auntie and Richard, an encounter of wills that would shape the course of our lives. "I'm ready to die," my auntie shouted, as she stood there staring down the barrel of the shotgun.

Suddenly, my brother, sister, and I were on our feet, propelled by a survival instinct we had no idea we possessed. We dashed out of our yard, down the street, and across the ditch. Our hearts pounded in our chests as fear and adrenaline coursed through our veins.

I am unable to remember every detail of how I got home that day. I recall stumbling through the front door, disoriented and dizzy, only to discover my bags and suitcase packed and ready for me. Ms. Lady had arranged for me to spend the summer with my uncle D and his wife.

Richard stayed, a dark cloud still hanging over our home.

RICHARD'S DEATH

I do not remember the exact events that prompted Ms. Lady to take us to the hospital, but I will never forget why we were there...

To visit Richard before he died.

I don't remember the exact year, but I remember finding myself grappling with emotions I never expected to face—a journey that led me to the bedside of the person who had caused me unbearable pain. As I stood there in the hospital, facing my abuser, I couldn't help but feel a whirlwind of conflicting emotions surge within me.

I bore the scars of the abuse he inflicted on me in the depths of my soul. The wounds may not be visible to the outside world, but they are deep and ingrained in the very fabric of who I am. I thought I had buried the hurt, anger, and fear, but seeing him lying there, frail and vulnerable, brought back a flood of memories and emotions.

Part of me wanted to turn away, to deny him the presence of someone he had previously tormented. It was tempting to abandon him to his fate, to absolve myself of any responsibility to care. Another part of me wanted revenge, to inflict the appropriate amount of suffering, pain, and agony comparable to what he put me through. But another part of me felt compelled to confront the demons of my past and stand up to the person who had tried to break me.

But then, I saw a reflection of my pain in his eyes. It served as a stark reminder that he was a broken soul, capable of causing pain because he, too, was in pain. I felt a slight twinge of empathy at that moment, realizing that our paths had diverged, and while I had chosen the path of healing, he had chosen the path of darkness.

The conflicting emotions kept tugging at my heart. I wanted to hate him for everything he had done, to keep the rage burning inside. But I also realized that hatred and anger were heavy burdens to bear, and I'd been carrying them for far too long. Forgiveness seemed impossible, but it beckoned, urging me to break free from the bonds of resentment.

When I think about that day, seeing Richard in the hospital was not my choice, and it was not an act of forgiveness. I realize it was just me at a young age trying to recognize my development, resilience, and ability to find compassion in the face of adversity. It was an opportunity to heal myself and recognize the broken soul before me, but I found it difficult to do, so I stuffed my pain.

As I walked out of that hospital room, I couldn't comprehend how far my recovery would be from being over. But somehow, I knew that I was stronger than I once thought and that I had the ability to shape my own story.

TIME MOVES FORWARD

As I progressed through my early teens, I became entangled in a web of emotions and confusion that seemed impossible to unravel. A love-hate relationship with men had taken root within me, shaped by the actions of two people who should have been pillars of support in my life.

The seeds of this complicated relationship were sown. My uncle, who had always been a reliable figure in my life, betrayed that trust in a thrashing way. His decision to rape me shattered my innocence and made me question all men's motives. I began associating them with deception and hurt.

Richard, followed suit with his own betrayal. His repeated molestations and beatings only added to my skepticism about the male gender. It felt as if the world had conspired to teach me that men were untrustworthy and capable of causing enormous pain. My only way of defending myself from them was by erecting barriers around my heart, determined not to let anyone in.

While I had grown to dislike men in general, I couldn't help but notice a stark contrast in Ms. Lady's way of life. She was never without a man by her side, and our house felt like a revolving door of male companions. And despite their transient presence in our lives, Ms. Lady seemed to find comfort and happiness in the company of these men.

You'd think witnessing her numerous relationships would have solidified my dislike of men, but the truth was far more complicated. I couldn't deny that she seemed happy while with a man, as if having a man by her side filled a void, a void she couldn't fill on her own. Reluctantly, I kept a close eye on her, trying to grasp the allure of these relationships.

On the other hand, my auntie stood in contrast to Ms. Lady's turbulent romantic life. My auntie was married to a man who genuinely cared about her. Their house was a haven of love and happiness, contrasting the chaos that frequently reigned in ours. My aunt's stable marriage and how they built a life together inspired me and left a lasting impression.

Growing up with such opposing influences, I was bound to form my opinions about relationships. I began associating having a man in my life with happiness, mirroring Ms. Lady's experiences. I yearned for the security and comfort that my aunt found in her marriage, but my reservations about men remained.

I was torn between these opposing emotions. I yearned for the happiness I imagined a man could bring into my life, but on the other end, I struggled to let go of the fear and distrust that had been instilled in me.

As I entered high school, I began dating in the hopes of finding the kind of love and security that my aunt had. But each relationship confirmed my earlier concerns. My trust was repeatedly betrayed, and I grew increasingly resentful of the men who had entered my life. I yearned for the joy I saw in my aunt's marriage, but it seemed increasingly elusive.

While searching for love and happiness, I frequently found myself in turbulent relationships, mirroring Ms. Lady's pattern. Even though I desperately wanted to change things, I couldn't break free from the cycle. It felt like I was caught in a never-ending battle between my desire for love and my deep mistrust of men.

In the following chapters, I navigate the rugged terrain of love and trust, attempting to reconcile my conflicting feelings with my father, men and the deeply held belief that having a man by my side was the key to my happiness. The road ahead was hazy, but I was determined to forge my path to love and fulfillment, hoping it would lift me out of the shadows of my past.

ENTERING HIGH SCHOOL

It's funny how fate's twists and turns often take us to unexpected places.

High school was not where I had envisioned to find myself, but it became a critical turning point in my journey. The abuse had left scars that lasted well into my adolescence, and I struggled to find peace and focus. My mind was constantly on the verge of spinning out of control, and it was a constant battle to keep my thoughts in check.

Keeping up with my studies was one of the most difficult challenges at the time, as Ms. Lady had never put my education first. She had her demons to battle, and I frequently bounced around schools and homes with no absolute consistency. Now that I was in high school, it was obvious that I was at an academic disadvantage.

High school should have been a time of opportunity and growth for me, but it turned into an uphill battle. I couldn't concentrate in class, and my attempts to study were always futile. The words and numbers on the pages seemed to mock me, dancing around and refusing to make sense. It was surprising I'd transitioned from elementary to junior high, and from junior high to high school with such a lack of educational skills.

It wasn't until much later that the puzzle pieces of my difficulties began to fit together. A concerned teacher suggested that I be tested for learning disabilities. It was a complex process, full of evaluations and assessments, but it was eventually determined that I had dyslexia. At the time, the word itself meant little to me, and no one really explained what it meant. All I knew was that it was somehow to blame for the chaos that ensued whenever I attempted to read or write.

This newfound knowledge stirred a strange mix of relief and embarrassment within me. I was relieved because it explained my difficulties; but I was embarrassed because it felt like a label, something distinct that differentiated me from my peers; and although I was placed into remedial classes, I kept it a secret close to my chest, afraid of the judgment and ridicule that might come if anyone found out.

That terror consumed me. I spent a lot of effort avoiding situations where I might be asked to read something aloud. I'd avoid group study sessions and reading assignments like the plague. I became an expert at making excuses and concealing my flaws. I'd silently pray that the teacher wouldn't call on me, and if they did, I'd mumble my way through, pretending to need glasses because the words on the page were too small.

As a result, my social life suffered. I kept my distance from people, never letting anyone get too close. It was safer to be the quiet one in the corner, blending in, than to risk being noticed. The thought of someone discovering my secret haunted me at all hours of the day and night.

Nevertheless, despite my struggles, something incredible happened one day. Somehow, amid my self-imposed isolation, I attracted the attention of my first boyfriend.

THE LOSS OF MY FIRST TWO LOVES

I had become the type of person who would rather blend in than stand out.

My self esteem (or lack thereof) was like a shroud that kept the world at bay. Even in a crowded room, I sat in my isolated bubble, a space where I could move around without being noticed. But life has a funny way of catching you off guard and throwing you a curve ball when you least expect it.

I first met him on a crisp autumn afternoon. His eyes were as warm and welcoming as the sun's golden rays, and his genuine and infectious smile immediately drew my attention. He attended a different high school, and he was a couple of years older than I, yet I found myself mesmerized by his vibrant tales of childhood and family. His upbringing utterly contrasted with my tumultuous past, which I kept tightly locked away, a heavy secret I hadn't yet shared.

He came from a loving family—his parents encouraged his creativity and supported his dreams. I loved listening to him recount his adventures with siblings and the warmth of their family gatherings, as if I could experience those moments vicariously through his words.

I began to live for our conversations, eagerly anticipating each shared experience. We'd spend hours discussing our favorite songs, movies, or simply sitting in comfortable silence. His presence soothed my hurting soul, a gentle reminder that I deserved happiness as well.

He told stories about challenges he'd faced and how he'd overcome them. I listened intently, learning from his experiences and being inspired by his tenacity. That's when I realized how much I admired him—not only for his kindness and understanding but also for his strength and determination.

Our friendship grew into something more as time passed. The fragile glow within me grew brighter as the possibility of love illuminated it. He saw something valuable in me, and for the first time, I began to see it as well.

But, as they say, life is unpredictable.

It was a bright morning when my heart witnessed the devastation that would forever change my life. The gentle rays of the sun streamed through the window, casting a warm glow on the bathroom wall.

My body and soul encountered an unexpected hurricane during those early weeks, leaving me caught in the crosshairs of life's unpredictability. My pregnancy had come as a delightful surprise, a testament to the love my adolescent heart had shared with a young man who had become my rock in this turbulent world. Our love story was a melody of innocence and discovery.

But fate can turn even the most beautiful melodies into sorrowful ballads. As the pregnancy progressed, a shadow began to cast itself over the canvas of our future together. An empty echo where our unborn child's rhythmic heartbeat should have been. The devastation hung heavy in the air, like an anchor sunk deep within my chest.

The days that followed were a blur of tears and unanswerable questions. A miscarriage? What had I mistakenly done? Why had my body betrayed me and taken my sliver of hope?

Amid this emotional storm, another one raged—a divide between my teenage love and me. Perhaps he couldn't find the right words to console me, or maybe the weight of our shared grief was too much for him to bear. Our conversations became distant, our once-shared secrets now obscured by silence.

He finally found the courage to speak during a quiet afternoon. His words cut through the warmth we had created like a blade. He stated that his father informed him that we could no longer continue to see one another. He couldn't explain why, only that his father demanded our relationship to end.

My heart shattered, and the light within me flickered, threatening to extinguish. Our shared memories, laughter, and dreams felt cruelly illusory at the time. I had allowed myself to believe in the possibility of happiness, only to have it snatched away from me.

I never told him about my traumatic childhood, my struggles with reading, or the internal battles I waged. Perhaps if I had been more open, more vulnerable, he would have understood the shadows that occasionally obscured my soul. But maybe some parts of us are too afraid to be seen, too fearful of the rejection that vulnerability might bring.

As I picked up the pieces of my heart, I realized that life had handed me another lesson. Sometimes, despite our best efforts and the beauty we find in others, relationships have their own mysterious rhythms. People come and go, leaving behind imprints on our hearts.

I found myself navigating not only the complicated web of grieving the loss of my child but also the perplexing maze of a teetering relationship. The love that had once linked us began to break, like frail threads slipping through my grasp. Our collective pain felt like a force field, repelling the intimate connection that had once been our sanctuary. Our shared hopes for the future now felt like a cruel joke, a mockery of destiny's cruel twist.

I fluctuated between wishing for a different life and grappling with the reality developing in front of me. Mourning the loss of a future with my child was excruciatingly painful, whereas the demise of my first romance as a teenager gnawed at my soul in an entirely different way. I stared at the sunset, its colors reminding me that even the most beautiful moments can fade away.

My wounds began to heal over time, but scars remained—etched reminders of what used to be and what could have been. I accepted our division, finding refuge in the memories that had brought us together and the snippets of life that slipped away.

MOMMA'S BOY AND GRADUATION

My heart skipped a beat the first time he smiled at me. I couldn't believe someone like him would even notice my presence. It was as if the sun had emerged from behind the clouds, warming my soul with a newfound sense of belonging. It was enticing, and I craved more.

I remember the first time I saw him. His perfect head full of curls and high yellow skin tone echoed the 1980s R&B singer El Debarge's charming style. The likeness was pleasing to my eyes, and my heart did a little somersault, setting the tone for what was to come.

The loss of my first two loves drove me to him and we began talking. I convinced myself that if he chose me, it would prove that I was deserving and important. His attention equaled validation in my mind, and that was all I desired. I convinced myself that being his girlfriend would solve everything and fill the void within me.

I found myself helplessly falling in love with the high school basketball star. Every time our gazes met, his athletic prowess and charismatic smile awoken a warm feeling in my heart. I had no idea that our love story would take unexpected twists and turns, leading me down the path of motherhood and heartbreak.

In the meantime, high school had been a maze of words and letters, a place where I was constantly at a loss. Although I was placed in remedial learning classes, dyslexia held me captive, denying me the ease of reading, spelling, and writing.

Every day was a battle, trying to decipher the code that others seemed to understand so quickly. While they easily wrote essays and read textbooks, I found myself drowning in a sea of jumbled symbols and misplaced sentences.

I attended Bullard High, a highly regarded school in our town. The halls echoed with the footsteps of ambitious students; each chasing dreams illuminated by the glow of knowledge. I felt like a shadow among them, silently drifting my way through an academic world that remained elusive and intimidating.

Teachers frequently misjudged my abilities, assuming I was simply uninterested or lazy. I did my best to keep up, seeking assistance and support wherever possible.

However, my determination was frequently outweighed by frustration and humiliation. I felt like I was always falling behind, unable to bridge the gap between my potential and the harsh reality of dyslexia.

Eventually, graduation day came and went, promising both closure and a ray of hope. I was surprised to see my name on the list of high school graduates.

Given the obstacles I faced over four years, it was an unexpected accomplishment.

I felt a mixture of confusion, pride and relief as I held that diploma in my hands. I felt pride as this was proof that I had persevered in the face of seemingly

insurmountable odds, but also confused because I still couldn't read or write very well. Regardless, I proudly walked across that stage, now pregnant with my second child.

I optimistically stepped into the world beyond, looking forward to life with my new love. Our love seemed unbreakable, and the prospect of a future together filled me with hope and excitement.

Unfortunately, shortly after the birth of our first daughter, Kay, it became clear that he was deeply rooted in his role as a momma's boy. His mother's opinions and demands weighed heavier than mine, resulting in a constant struggle for his love and attention. My once loving and attentive partner began to prioritize his mother's wishes over our family's responsibilities.

I soon found myself caught in the middle, torn between my feelings for him and my feelings for our newborn daughter. I tried to bridge the gap time and time again, hoping for compromise and understanding. Despite my best efforts, his mother's influence always seemed stronger.

The load of unmet expectations and unfulfilled promises weighed heavily on our relationship. The love that had once been a beacon of hope faded, leaving a painful void in its wake. I had to confront the heartbreaking reality that our relationship would not survive.

With a heavy heart, I made the difficult decision to part ways, realizing that the well-being of Kay was more important. It was a terrifying leap into the unknown, but I knew deep down that it was the right decision. I needed to find the courage to raise our daughter alone.

My relationship with Ms. Lady was still chaotic and Kay's father's involvement in her life was becoming more infrequent. On one occasion, Kay's father had come to visit, and for a reason I can't recall, we began to argue. The argument became progressively worse causing Ms. Lady to enter the room and intervene. She never asked what the altercation was about, but she told Momma's Boy he could stay... and I had to leave; she told me to get on the phone and find somewhere else to live.

Kay was 3 months old at this time, so I desperately tried to call several different "friends" and family members seeking shelter for myself and my newborn, but time and time again I was denied.

Finally, in a last-ditch effort, I called an uncle and spoke to his wife. I explained my circumstances to her, and she said that my daughter and I could come and live with them. I was immensely grateful but could not grasp the magnitude of how fortunate I was.

Living with my uncle, time seemed to fly by. Kay was now two years old, but Mama's Boy remained firm in his refusal to accept his responsibilities as a father.

Our most heated argument took place within the walls of his mother's home. I had brought Kay for a visit, and he was annoyed by my unannounced arrival, telling me I should have called ahead of time.

His mother, heard the altercation and told me to take my baby and leave her home. I returned to my uncle's house shaking with unbearable anger. Distraught, I called Ms. Lady and told her to care for my daughter. I grabbed my prescription of iron pills and took the entire bottle.

The next thing I remember was waking up in the hospital several days later. The hospital discharged me back to my uncle's house and as soon as I was well enough, my uncle's wife took me to look for an apartment of my own. What I had done was never discussed but I knew I had overstayed my welcome after my suicide attempt.

ON MY OWN

I was now thrust into a terrifying reality, navigating life's storm with only determination and the fierce love I had for my daughter. Life had dealt me an intricate hand, leaving me alone and insecure in my first apartment, clinging to the tenuous hope that things would improve.

The little apartment that became our refuge was made possible by my uncle's wife, who, despite evicting me from her home after my suicide attempt, extended a lifeline by assisting in securing this roof over our heads.

As the days turned into weeks, my fear and anxiety began to fade, and were gradually replaced by a sense of responsibility and a fierce maternal instinct. I was alone, but my little Kay required my assistance. I was terrified, but that fear fueled my desire to be the mother I had never known.

We scraped by with the help of welfare and food stamps, but it was never about just scraping by. It was about giving my daughter the best life I could despite the circumstances. I spent what little money I had on age-appropriate learning games and books. It was my way of laying the groundwork for a brighter future, where she could thrive and exceed all expectations.

Every day was a lesson in perseverance and creativity. I'd cradle my daughter gently while holding a book on my lap. The ABCs became a daily ritual for us. Battling my dyslexia, I whispered the letters to her in a tender, melodic voice as I too practiced those fundamental building blocks of spelling. It was a symphony of hope, a promise that her education, world, and love would be different, that she would have the opportunities and affection I was denied.

The pages of children's books turned into gateways of learning, adventure and imagination. Kay would laugh as I animated the characters, attempting to convey the magic within each story. Most of the time, I'd stumble over the words, still learning myself, but it never deterred me. It was about the act of reading, the shared experience, and the bond I was forging.

With each turn of the page, I could feel our bond strengthening like a fragile sapling growing against all odds. It was a reminder that no matter how daunting the world seemed or the struggles we faced, love and determination could illuminate the darkest corners of our lives.

I persisted despite sleepless nights and tiring mornings. In her innocence, Kay was blissfully unaware of the difficulties we were facing. She giggled and clapped, her laughter filling our tiny apartment with a warmth I had never known. By the time Kay was three, she could recite the alphabet, count to twenty and knew all 50 states by sight.

I held her close one evening as the horizon painted the sky in a soft pink hue. As I softly recited the words, she clutched a brightly colored book, her gaze fixed on the pictures. My love for this tiny being overwhelmed me, and tears rose in my eyes.

I realized at that moment, despite the difficulties, we were creating a beautiful life together. She was my ray of hope, guiding me through the storm and reminding me that the sun would come out again and that the hardships were worth every precious moment spent with her.

LEE

Kay, now nearly four years old, was a constant reminder of the passage of time and the dreams that tugged at my heart. I had always imagined a fairy tale life for myself: a lovely home with a white picket fence, a devoted husband, and a happy family. Despite the unhealed wounds of my past, I longed for that dream, hoping that love could rewrite the script of my existence.

Life had been a rollercoaster since my previous relationship ended. The wounds were still raw, and the echoes of betrayal and heartbreak haunted my thoughts. However, Kay's innocence and laughter helped me bury those painful memories, at least for a while. I knew deep down that I hadn't dealt with my past properly, but the overwhelming responsibilities of motherhood didn't leave much time for introspection.

Kay demanded my attention and love with her bright eyes and infectious giggles. I clung to every ounce of joy she brought into my life as I made my way through motherhood. When I saw her smile, and felt her tiny arms wrapped around me in a warm embrace, the late nights and early mornings, tears and tantrums were all worth it.

But from time to time, there were quiet moments when the bustle of daily life faded, and I found myself wrestling with my own desires and dreams. My auntie's life had always been a source of inspiration for me. She had everything I desired: a home, a husband, a family and a love that was the epitome of joy. It was the kind of life sold to us in romantic movies, a life that felt like a distant mirage.

I yearned for that kind of love—a love that would heal my past wounds, a love that would complete our little family. My heart ached, as I fantasized about a man who would come into our lives, sweep me off my feet, and adore Kay as if she were his own.

Then, one day, without looking for him, we met. We started a conversation that flowed naturally like we'd known each other for years. He was gentle, compassionate, and open about his own struggles and triumphs. He'd been through heartbreak and disappointment, but his resilience shone through. As our friendship grew, I felt a glimmer of hope that this could be the start of the love story I had imagined.

But deep down, the scars of my past still throbbed. I had not fully addressed the pain and insecurities gnawing at my soul.

For years, I carried the weight of my painful past—rape, molestation, beatings, broken relationships, betrayal, and heart-break. My experiences made me, time after time, doubt my worth and my ability to recognize genuine love when it appeared.

I now found myself in a relationship with Lee, a man who seemed to shine like a light in the darkness. He was thoughtful, compassionate and he lavished me with affection. But in all honestly, I couldn't fully comprehend the depth of his love. My perception was clouded by the remnants of my past wounds, leading me to doubt his intentions and fear that history would repeat itself.

Love had become synonymous with pain in my mind, a bittersweet symphony that had left me guarded and hesitant to embrace affection. I had built walls around my heart in the hope that they would protect me from further pain. However, by doing so, I missed out on the love I had longed for.

As our relationship grew, I found myself pushing him away. We had now been together for some years and at this time, I had the birth of my second daughter; and although I had given Lee a child, I began putting distance between us because I was afraid, he would hurt me too. I did not realize that my subconscious wounds were unintentionally sabotaging what could have been a lovely love story.

For the first few years, he was patient. As he learned about my past, he saw through my defenses and recognized the pain I was carrying. He held me close, promising to be there for me through thick and thin, and I believed in the forever we had imagined together. But our relationship's dynamics began to shift along the way, and the love that had once flourished began to wither.

I was burdened by a past that had left its imprint on my heart and soul and as our relationship developed, my emotional scars proved too much for him to bear.

Over time, I started to see the glint of resentment in his eyes, the disappointment that my past difficulties were not easily erased. I tried everything I could to work through my issues and communicate openly with him, but the heaviness of my pain had started to weigh down on him too.

Slowly, our union evolved into something unrecognizable yet all too familiar. As we both turned to verbal and, eventually, physical abuse as outlets for our growing resentment. The very relationship I desired became a breeding ground for toxicity, hate, and pain.

At first, the signs of abuse were subtle—a harsh word, a dismissive comment—but it gradually turned darker and more sinister as his once loving and open hands became balled-up fists of rage and fury. I tried to justify his actions, trying to convince myself deep down that he still loved me. But I eventually realized I was stuck in an abusive cycle, and I couldn't seem to pull myself out; and just when I thought things couldn't get any worse, came a conversation that would forever change the way I would feel about Lee. A conversation I could never have imagined having.

THE LOSS OF
MY THIRD LOVE

It's strange how life can shift suddenly, like tectonic plates beneath the earth's surface. One moment, you're gliding through the days with a sense of certainty and then the ground beneath you shakes, leaving you in a state of disarray. I never expected to be at this crossroads, face to face with the man I once thought would be my husband and partner for life.

As I sit down to write this chapter of my life, my heart is heavy with memories of a time when trust was broken and love took on a new, painful meaning. The day he said those words, the request that seemed to shatter my dreams is etched in my memory like a bruise that will never fade...

Our daughter, Shay, my second child, was asleep. I watched her quietly, wrapped in the indescribable warmth that comes from witnessing a little human grow before your eyes. She represented the love we had once shared, a testament to the bond we had formed in the early years of our relationship. However, those early years were now being overshadowed by something darker.

I recall the atmosphere in the room shifting as Lee carefully selected his words, his face bearing an unsettling mix of desperation and cold determination. "I want you to get an abortion."

It felt as if the ground beneath me had crumbled, leaving me suspended in an emotional abyss. The father of our child, who had promised to stand by my side, was now requesting that I erase a part of myself to satisfy his desires. I sat there, dumbfounded, trying to comprehend the enormity of his request. How could he expect me to make such a decision?

I was caught in a whirlwind of emotions; treachery, rage, and a painful sadness that gnawed at my heart. I was hurt not only by his request for an abortion but also by the calmness he presented, which turned out to be a stark revelation of his true character. How could he so callously discard the second life we had created together? Was this the man I'd known? I felt as if I had been blind to the reality that was unfolding in front of me.

Watching our innocent and oblivious daughter sleep only heightened the turbulent storm within me. I couldn't understand how he could look at our daughter and request such a sacrifice. It was as if our dreams had collided with the jagged rocks of reality, leaving only shards of what could have been.

Ultimately, I got the abortion…

Following that decision, my thoughts turned into a raging hurricane within the confines of my mind. My constant companions were a whirlwind of emotions ranging from relief to guilt, grief to anger. The relief came from a sense of practicality, terribly aware that without the support and stability I needed, I couldn't provide the life I wanted for my daughters. But tangled within that relief was a knot of guilt, a devastating suspicion that I had betrayed a part of myself.

As the days turned into weeks, resentment slipped in, casting a shadow over the love I had once shared with Lee. Our relationship now bore the weight of a decision that had divided us in unexpected ways. It was as if the bond we had woven had frayed at the edges, unraveling thread by thread.

It wasn't a sudden collapse; rather, it was a gradual deterioration of the foundation we had built. Small disagreements became explosive fights. The love we had once shared seemed like a distant memory, a relic of a time before our lives had been turned upside down by a single request.

As I moved through the emotional terrain, I realized that my resentment wasn't solely directed at him. It was also directed at myself for allowing outside pressures to influence a decision to sacrifice a part of me for the sake of practicality.

LEAVING LEE, THE FIGHT

The day came when I "found" my reason to break free from the suffocating bond of Lee, a relationship tainted by violence, an abortion request, and now a heartbreaking cultural betrayal.

For a long time, I suffered hoping that things would get better. However, hope alone cannot repair what someone is unwilling to confront. I tried to persevere and find a solution, motivated by my desire not to repeat Ms. Lady's long resume of partners. I fought hard not to conform to stereotypical portrayals of Black women having numerous children with numerous men. Above all, I was terrified of being alone and without anyone to love and support me.

But as the layers of abuse were peeled away, I discovered a heartbreaking truth that slashed deeply into my identity as an African-American woman. Lee was being unfaithful; he had been cheating on me, secretly seeing a woman of a different race. Infidelity is a betrayal in and of itself, but the added layer of cultural betrayal struck a deep chord within my soul.

I couldn't help but wonder if he saw me as insufficient. Was it because of my painful past that I was deemed unworthy? The questions swirled around in my head, and my heart ached with a different sense of loss and rejection I'd never felt before.

My trust was shattered. A white woman? Although she was of mixed nationality, she was not black! She didn't look like me. She didn't look like his daughter! The pain of infidelity is enough to break a person's spirit on its own, but the added layer of race magnifies the pain to an extent I never expected.

My partner, the man whom I birthed a daughter, betrayed me through infidelity, and the revelation carries a profound cultural complexity that I couldn't ignore. The revelation heightened when I learned that they met through a mutual male friend whom we both trusted and this male friend too, was a black man. The sense of betrayal had extended beyond my relationship. In hindsight, I should have known better, for our mutual male friend, was also dating a white woman.

The Fight…

I sat on the edge of the couch, waiting for Lee's return, my heart filled with rage, betrayal, and a tinge of desperation. My thoughts raced with images of Lee with another woman while claiming to be "working" on our relationship. I thought about all the "evening shifts" he told me he was scheduled to work; it was a crushing weight on my chest just thinking about it.

I glanced at the wall clock, it's face mocking me with each passing minute. Lee, once again, was late, and anxiety gnawed at my insides. My thoughts spiraled, and I had to fight to keep them in check. The confrontation that awaited seemed insurmountable, a behemoth of pain and anger.

The front door creaked open, jolting me to attention. My pulse quickened, and my hands trembled as I clenched them into fists, bracing for the inevitable storm. Lee walked in, his face mirroring exhaustion from a day's work, oblivious to the storm that awaited him.

He looked at me, his eyes widening with surprise and perhaps a hint of guilt. "Hey, baby," he greeted cautiously.

"You bastard," I said, my voice sharp and composed. I had rehearsed this confrontation in my mind a thousand times but facing him was another story.

He closed the front door, concern etched across his face. "Is everything okay?" he asked.

"Okay? No, Lee, nothing is okay," I seethed, trying to steady my voice. "What's going on?" he asked.

"I found out, Lee. I found out about her, I found out about your other woman," I shouted, the words heavy on my tongue, each one a hammer driving a wedge between us. His face paled, and his eyes darted around, unable to meet mine. He was trapped in his deceit, caught in the act.

"You've been seeing her, pretending to work on our relationship, pretending everything was going to be fine between us! How could you?" My voice quivered with a blend of hurt and disbelief.

He finally met my gaze, his eyes shifting from remorse to an odd defiance. "It's not what you think," he attempted weakly.

"What the hell is it then? Please, enlighten me, what the hell is it?" I demanded.

Anger and rage consumed me, fueled by the inadequacy of his excuses. We've been together for years. I gave you a daughter! You asked me to get an abortion! How could you!" Tears welled up, but I blinked them away, refusing to let them fall in front of him.

The argument escalated into a whirlwind of accusations, pushing, shoving, hurtful truths, and shattered promises. It was a battlefield where my body and trust lay shredded, gasping for breath. The confrontation left us both physically battered and emotionally exhausted, the reality of our broken relationship now undeniable.

As the night wore on, I was pushed to confront the harsh reality that the love I had once held so close had crumbled beneath the weight of deceit. It was a painful truth, but it was necessary for me to reclaim the shattered pieces of my heart and attempt to rebuild the strength to move forward.

Looking back on that chapter of my life, I can't help but question my judgment, and the genuineness of the connections I thought were solid. The pain was overwhelming, and I grappled once again with self-doubt, asking whether I was enough in all aspects of my life.

MEETING MY FATHER

Psychosis has a cruel way of robbing you of memories and important details. Some recollections are crystal clear, etched in my mind like a vivid painting, while others seem to have faded into the hazy corners of forgetfulness. My encounter with my father falls into the latter category, a moment that left me with more questions than answers.

I can't pinpoint the exact details of that day. Was it sunny or overcast? Were we at my grandmother's home or Ms. Lady's? And why had my father returned to Fresno, California? It's all a blur, lost in the fog caused my battles with mental illness. But what I do remember, with a sharp clarity that cuts through the haze, is the profound disappointment that lingered in the air after our reunion.

I can still feel the surreal sensation as if I were looking at a stranger rather than the man who was supposed to be in my life. The prospect of coming face-to- face with him had always been as exciting as terrifying. But now that I was an adult, all those hopes for a loving reunion seemed to have crumbled.

Throughout my childhood, I had wished to meet my father, a distant figure shrouded in mystery. Ms. Lady never said much about him, yet, on occasion, I imagined how our meeting would go; a loving father finally embracing his long- lost daughter. I had no idea that reality had something completely different in store for me.

I will never forget the first time we laid eyes on each other; I couldn't stop staring at him. His eyes briefly met mine, but there was no sign of recognition or warmth in them. I tried to smile, hoping to bridge the gap, but he averted his gaze as if I were an inconvenient reminder of a time he'd rather forget. It seemed like the world stood still. I studied every feature of his face, his stance, muscle tone, and beautiful caramel skin complexion; It was like looking into a mirror. My goodness, he was a beautiful man.

My father did not say anything at first; he just stared at me the way I was staring at him, but I was gazing at him through the eyes of a 5-year-old girl who desperately needed her father's love. He was staring at me, studying my features, to see if I looked anything like him, only to validate if I were his daughter.

The study session seemed to last a lifetime; neither of us said anything. We just stood in silence, and then, without a word, my father turned around and left the room, only to return a few seconds later with a photograph. He handed me the picture, a snapshot of him in high school. I immediately became filled with emotion because it was like I was staring at my own high school photograph.

The silence was broken when my father said, "Don't tell my mother I came to Fresno." He turned and walked away.

As I walked away from that encounter, I realized that the absence of a father's love had shaped me in various ways. But I also knew that somewhere deep inside, it had made me stronger and more resilient. I didn't need his approval to prove my worth.

As difficult as it was to accept, I realized that some bonds were never meant to be repaired, and with a heavy heart, I never sought my father again.

MOVING BACK HOME WITH MS. LADY

After parting with Lee, I decided to leave the apartment that we once shared. I could not come to grips with the painful memories etched into the walls of a place we once called home. Plus, I found myself facing the challenge of being on my own once again, except now, I have two daughters. My circumstances had become difficult, and we needed a temporary place to stay. I had an eviction on my credit report so finding a place of my own was going to be impossible. Against my better judgment, I reached out to Ms. Lady. It was a reluctant decision, but she had a spacious two-bedroom, one-and-a-half-bathroom, two-story town house where she resided alone. I explained my situation and asked if we could stay there until I found a stable job and regained our footing. Surprisingly, she responded, "You can come whenever you want and stay for as long as you need." While her enthusiasm struck me as unusual, I was simply grateful that my children and I had a roof over our heads, no longer facing the prospect of living in my small jeep.

The following month, I rented a mini storage and stowed away all my valuable furniture and belongings. I carefully selected only the essentials: my kids' beds and clothes. During one weekday while Ms. Lady was at work, I moved us into her home and started to settle in. When Ms. Lady returned, her initial enthusiastic smile faded into discontent as she took in her townhome's altered appearance. "Where is everything?" she demanded to know.

Confused, I asked, "What do you mean?"

She raised her voice, "The furniture! Where is all the furniture?" As she wandered through her house, she meticulously observed and questioned, "Where's your loveseat, couch, and ottoman? Where is your big oil painting and the border that matches the furniture? Where's your black ceiling fan, black entertainment center, deep freezer, and large TV?"

I calmly explained that I had placed all unnecessary items in storage, bringing only what we needed. But Ms. Lady insisted on having everything at her place. It became evident that she had allowed us to stay, expecting me to bring my nice furniture and belongings.

Despite my reservations, I found myself in a difficult predicament. And so, eventually, I agreed and brought everything she requested.

A few weeks later, Ms. Lady informed me that the landlord had discovered my daughters and me living there without being on the rental agreement. The landlord told her we would have to leave. I asked if it was possible to add us to the rental agreement and offered to pay the necessary deposit. After a moment of silence, Ms. Lady informed me that she had already inquired, and the answer was no. "Okay," I responded, "I'll start looking for a new place to live."

In a feeble attempt to reassure me, Ms. Lady said, "You can leave all your stuff here; I'll take care of them for you." I didn't acknowledge her last statement, my mind racing with distrust. Instead, I turned and began walking upstairs, mumbling under my breath, "You must be a fool if you think I'm leaving my belongings here with you." The uncertainty of our situation weighed heavily on my shoulders, but my determination to secure a stable and safe environment for my children pushed me forward.

I began a desperate search for a new apartment, my sights set on a place to call home, but fate had other plans. Every prospective landlord I approached turned down my rental applications. An eviction from years ago loomed over my record, threatening my chances of finding a place to live. Ms. Lady would pester me every week, asking about my progress in finding a new place to live.

"Have you found a place yet?" She would inquire, her concern evident in her tone of voice.

"Not yet," I'd say, growing increasingly discouraged.

"Well, you need to hurry up; the landlord is giving me a hard time about you being here."

It struck me as odd that the landlord, whenever I encountered her, maintained a friendly demeanor and never brought up the subject of my living situation with Ms. Lady. After a brief pause, I realized I hadn't seen the landlord in months, but the search for a place to live continued.

After a month of dealing with my housing crisis, I applied to the County of Fresno for emergency housing and general relief assistance. Fortunately, my application was approved. The program included a 30-day stay at the Knights Inn Motel, which was far from ideal but provided a roof over our heads. I returned to my storage, grateful that my daughters and I would not be homeless, to prepare for our upcoming move.

Later that evening, a burst of laughter surprised me as I approached the sliding patio door to enter Ms. Lady's home. When I walked in, I found Ms. Lady and her old boyfriend, Ernest, seated in the living room. Ernest, whom I had no idea had been released from prison, was there at Ms. Lady's invitation, which sent shivers up my spine.

I responded to their greetings and exchanged pleasant-ries with Ernest while trying to maintain my composure. The scene was unsettling; Ms. Lady, sitting on Ernest's lap... on my love seat... under my ceiling fan... sipping drinks... enjoying my television! They seemed very comfortable.

"Ernest, do you remember my daughter?" Ms. Lady asked.

"Yes, I do! Hey Crystal, how are you doing?" Ernest in-quired, pretending to be sincere.

"I'm fine, and you?" I replied, trying not to lose my cool.

"Aww, I'm fine. I'm just glad to be home. Didn't your moth-er do a great job on the house?" Ernest remarked, adding to the surrealism of the moment.

I muttered, "Yes, her place is really nice." I turned and made my way upstairs, unable to deal with the mix of confu-sion, anger, and betrayal.

The following week, I organized the removal of all my be-longings from Ms. Lady's townhome, and my daughters and I moved into the motel. A few weeks after my departure, Ms. Lady offered our empty bedroom to my brother, allowing him to stay with her for a year, giving him time to pay off his dam-aged credit, buy new furniture, and save money for his own place.

When my brother moved out, Ms. Lady allowed my sister

and her two children to move in with her, providing them with a place to live indefinitely. This experience was a painful re-minder of Ms. Lady's true nature and a reminder of my dire need for self-reliance.

HOMELESS WITH TWO CHILDREN

I recall the day we checked into that motel, our only option for maintaining some semblance of stability for the next thirty days. The once-vibrant motel had seen better days, but it was a haven for us in that time of uncertainty. Our room was small but retained a unique charm, thanks to a mural on one of the walls depicting a peaceful forest with a gentle stream flowing through it.

As a mother, it became my mission to make our temporary residence an oasis for my daughters. I needed to make this feel like an adventure, like a camping trip, so they would be able to handle our situation. I saw the mural as a tool for weaving camping and nature stories into our daily lives. It was a lie, but it was woven with love and necessity.

The mornings were a blur. I'd get up early to ensure the girls were dressed and ready. After a 10-mile drive, we would arrive at their school, where they could eat breakfast. My day would then begin in earnest. Shopping for groceries, a small bag of chicken, a small bag of white rice, and a can of Campbell's Cream of Chicken Soup became the foundation of our meals.

The crockpot became my ally, a simple appliance that allowed me to prepare a warm, comforting dinner for my daughters while I worked long hours to make ends meet. I did my best to maintain the appearance of our "camping trip", to keep the darkness at bay and to give my children a sense of normalcy.

The afternoons and evenings were dedicated to making those thirty days as memorable and joyful as possible. After their homework was completed, hours were spent playing Uno, watching cartoons, and embracing the fleeting moments of happiness. My daughters, wrapped up in the illusion of a camping adventure, were blissfully unaware of our dire circumstances. They laughed and smiled, and for those precious moments, I felt like I was doing something right.

Time seemed to dance by, and our motel stay was over before we knew it. Then, the reality of our situation hit me hard—I had not found a solution, a way to provide a permanent home for my family. The burden of failure weighed heavy on my heart, but I couldn't let my daughters see my struggle. I was their mother, their pillar of strength, and I had to stay strong for them.

We moved into a homeless shelter for women on the west side of Fresno, where the starkness of the situation became even more apparent. It was a difficult time, and I struggled with depression, suicidal thoughts and feelings of inadequacy. I felt like I had failed my children by not being able to protect them from the harsh realities of life. But, through the darkness, I held on to hope.

I clung to that glimmer of hope for months and sometime later, I bumped into a family friend while running errands. He asked how I was doing, and after I explained my circumstances, he offered me a rent-free room in his home. It was an enormous gesture of kindness that afforded me an opportunity to rebuild our lives. I worked tirelessly, saving every penny to provide a better future for my daughters.

And nearly a year later, after what seemed like an eternity, I found us a small apartment. It wasn't much, but it was ours—a symbol of our fortitude and the love that had sustained us during our darkest hours. Our journey was far from over, but for the first time in a long time, I felt a glimmer of triumph, that I would be able to overcome the obstacles that life had thrown my way.

Nothing "Grand" in a Grandmother

Growing up, I always felt the chill of Ms. Lady's disapproval. It was like a cold breeze that could freeze even the happiest moments. And it wasn't just me; she held that same disdain for her own mother, my grandmother. I knew her contempt shaped how she saw the world and me, but I never expected it to reach my daughters, her own grandchildren.

For my two little girls, I had imagined balloons, cake, laughter, and the excitement of a grandmother's birthday wish. But as time passed, this all felt more like a fading whisper lost in the wind. No calls to sing "Happy Birthday," no cards in the mail with her unique handwriting, and no gifts wrapped in her loving style.

Birthdays and holidays felt incomplete for my girls—like a recipe missing a crucial ingredient: Grandma's touch. It's funny how absence can create such a tangible void, especially when you dearly wish someone would be part of your special moments.

Ms. lady's silence on their birthdays became the norm as years passed. But explaining this disconnection was like solving a puzzle with missing pieces. How do you tell your daughters that their grandmother doesn't love them? How do you rationalize into words the unexplainable gap between a grandmother and her granddaughters?

Christmas mornings held a different kind of sadness. The joy of the season was there, but there was also a tinge of disappointment. There were plenty of gifts under the tree, but none with grandma's name tag, and inevitably, this led to questions from my girls.

"Mom, why doesn't grandma call or send us anything?" or "Did she forget about us this Christmas?"

I tried to cover it up, making excuses that maybe Ms. Lady was busy or had her unique way of showing love. But in their innocent eyes, I saw their longing for her presence, for that unique connection only a grandmother can bring.

It wasn't just about the lack of material gifts; it was the absence of grandmotherly love—the stories, the comforting food, the warmth of her embrace—that left an echo in their hearts. They struggled to understand why their cousins got so much love and attention from grandma while they barely received anything.

As a mother, shielding your kids from disappointment is a priority, but this was one heartache I could not fix. And that hurt, watching their excitement dampen, trying to make sense of a love that seemed uneven—it's a feeling that lingers.

So, I attempted to bridge the gap one Christmas and mend the rift during the holidays. I told Ms. Lady how much my daughters missed their grandma and wished to spend the night, waking up with her on Christmas morning. But her response was a gentle refusal disguised as an offer—a short visit on Christmas Day, citing work obligations.

Christmas day soon arrived, and we went, my daughters eager to see their grandmother. But joy turned to a quiet sadness when they found out their cousins had spent the night. Their excitement faded as they realized the unequal treatment they received.

My sister's children ran up to us, happy, showing off their new clothes and toys. Their happiness was infectious. I pushed aside my hurt and showed genuine love and warmth toward them, not wanting my feelings to affect any child.

Then came the moment that crushed my daughters' hearts. Excitedly, my youngest asked Grandma about her gifts. Ms. Lady left the living room to get them, but what came back were two tiny boxes. Their excitement turned to tears as they opened these boxes to find twist-on plastic water bottle caps—

plain, unusable, ordinary items that should have been thrown in the trash.

It's a painful lesson that speaks volumes about family cycles and the unintended victims they leave behind. My daughters learned that sometimes the love they hope for might never be returned, no matter how much they wish for it. And that realization, that quiet understanding, broke my heart more than anything else.

THE CLASH OF A TITAN: MY HUSBAND JAMES

I fell in love with a man who appeared to embody my fantasies. Little did I know that this man would become my tormentor and savior against all odds.

The early days with my now husband was genuinely enchanting. I met him during the summer of 1992, and his charm was like a magnet, pulling me into a world of promises of a future filled with love and togetherness. His handsome smile lit up the darkest corners of my heart and staring at his chocolate covered skin made me feel like I had stumbled upon my knight in shining armor.

What made those early days even more beautiful was how he embraced me and my life without judgment. I was afraid, worried that my past would taint his perception of me. Two daughters, each from different fathers, and the struggles of living on welfare and food stamps had shaped my story. But he never made me feel less because of it.

I remember those times when my heart felt heavy with the weight of my own limitations. The inability to read or write felt like a secret I needed to hide. Yet, he never prodded or pushed. Instead, he wrapped me in patience and understanding.

What truly touched me, though, was his unwavering support for my daughters. Day in and day out, he'd sit with them, guiding them through their schoolwork,

especially their English assignments. The way he'd patiently explain things, breaking down complex concepts into simpler ones, meant the world to me. He'd never let frustration creep in, always encouraging them to do their best.

He wasn't just a boyfriend; he became a pillar of strength for me. His dedication to helping my girls thrive academically went beyond words. The way he believed in them, fostering their confidence was a gift I couldn't have asked for.

But the roads we travel turn and twist in ways we could never imagine. It wasn't like in the movies, where a sudden storm breaks everything apart. No, it was more like a slow unraveling, a gradual transformation that I couldn't quite grasp until it was too late.

That downward spiral began after a showdown that shook everything I knew right down to its core. Lee, was still in the picture thanks to a custody deal ordered by the court. Even though he'd moved on and crafted a new life, now engaged to the woman he cheated on me with, it seemed like my new-found happiness bothered him.

Lee was dead set on wrecking my new relationship, and things got ugly when he started clashing with James over the phone. Then, instead of picking up his daughter on scheduled days, Lee began to show up at my door, claiming he needed to get some personal belongings he had left behind... but it felt like he was just there to pick a fight.

The more Lee pushed, the more James brushed him off, which Lee took as a sign of weakness. Then, one night, all hell broke loose. During a scheduled visitation hand-off of our daughter, Lee did something I never imagined possible—he started an argument with me and shoved me into a wooden fence right in front of James.

That one act of disrespect on Lee's behalf was the key that unlocked the gates of hell.

The air crackled with tension as I watched, frozen in a blend of horror and disbelief. It was like witnessing a surreal transformation, an otherworldly shift that ripped the fabric of the familiar and unleashed something nightmarish.

James, the gentle soul I'd come to know, was locked in a brutal clash with my daughter's father. What had started with words over the phone now escalated into a physical confrontation that felt like a scene from a horror film.

I stood there, my heart pounding as if trapped in slow motion, watching as the most caring, loving man I knew began to change before my eyes. It wasn't just anger—it was as though his essence, the very core of his being, was stripped away, replaced by something unrecognizable.

What emerged was a torrent of rage, a fury so primal and intense that it felt like a force of nature. It was as if his humanity had left, leaving behind a raw, untamed beast that was all-consuming.

The violence that followed was beyond anything I could have imagined. Every blow felt like a collision of thunder and each strike tore through the air with a terrifying ferocity. James, or what remained of him at that moment, unleashed a savagery upon my ex that painted the parking lot with an unsettling shade of brutality.

At first, a part of me—the part that sought protection and defense—welcomed the sight of my boyfriend standing up for me without hesitation. But that feeling

quickly gave way to a chilling fear as I realized the depths of the abyss he had plummeted into.

I screamed, pleaded, and tried to intervene, but it was like trying to hold back a hurricane with bare hands. The violence seemed uncontainable, an unstoppable force tearing through everything in its path.

Deep in the pit of my stomach, a gnawing dread took hold. I feared not just for the safety of my daughter's father but for the man I loved, now unrecognizable in this maelstrom of rage. I feared that someone wouldn't make it out alive if this continued.

Desperation clawed at me as I sprinted upstairs to dial for help, to summon the authorities before the chaos swallowed everything whole. I prayed that they would arrive in time to prevent the irreversible.

As I trembled with the receiver in my hand, the echoes of the scene lingered like a haunting melody. It wasn't just a fight—it was a descent into a realm of horror, where the line between a man and something darker blurred in the most chilling way possible. After speaking with the authorities, I raced back downstairs only to find Lee stumbling to his car and leaving.

James emerged physically victorious from that altercation, but something had shifted within him. It was as though a piece of his soul had been ripped away, leaving behind a void that no amount of victory could fill. In the following months, he withdrew into himself, his laughter fading, replaced by a haunted look in his eyes that tore into my heart.

He became distant, his smiles becoming more forced, his touch, less comforting. There were nights when I'd find him staring into the darkness, lost in thoughts he couldn't—and wouldn't—share.

I wondered if the man I fell in love with was still in there, buried beneath layers of pain and unresolved emotions. I held onto hope, believing that time would heal the wound that had scarred our relationship. But as weeks became months, I couldn't shake the feeling that we were drifting apart, tethered together by memories of a summer, a time when everything felt right.

James's abuse began subtly, with a dismissive comment here and a controlling action there. It was as if the man I used to adore had been replaced by a stranger, someone consumed by their own demons and rage. I found myself walking on eggshells, desperate to avoid his wrath while clinging to the shards of love I once felt.

The emotional abuse became more intense with each passing year and as physical abuse began to set in, I sank to the bottom of a sea of fear and self-doubt, becoming a shell of my former self. Finding happiness again seemed like a distant memory, an unattainable dream.

Years later, I would find out that James was a mirror image of my own upbringing. The same broken family structure, the same lack of motherly love, and the same burden of being the eldest, feeling responsible for protecting his younger brother; if that weren't enough, James's childhood had been dark and sinister like mine.

His mother, who lacked maternal warmth, had been a source of terror rather than comfort for him. Her relentless abuse manifested itself in verbal assaults, emotional cruelty, mental torment, and physical violence. This malevolent force that should have been a nurturing presence tainted James's very existence. And if that were not enough, James was horrifically abused and tortured by a set of two stepfathers, who happened to be brothers.

As our relationship progressed, I learned about the demons that haunted James's past. He trusted me enough to tell me about his horrendous childhood experiences, recounting tales of pain and suffering that no child should bear. I could feel the weight of his words and the burdens he carried.

Despite the darkness, there was a glimmer of something pure... love. James's affection for me was genuine and deep. Despite the darkness that clouded his past and influenced his actions, I could see his passion for me trying to shine through. It was a love twisted and contorted by the horrors he had lived through, but it was still love.

That was the kind of love I recognized. It was the same love I carried in my heart, entangled in a web of painful memories. James and I were two wounded souls clinging to each other in a vast, lonely world.

Our relationship was turbulent, marked by battles with the ghosts of our respective pasts. It was a never-ending war, a stormy sea that threatened to consume us.

James's past had scarred him, and his actions sometimes mirrored the abuse he had endured. Despite the chaos, I saw glimpses of the man he could become, the man he desperately desired to be.

Then, during the darkest hour of my life, as I lay broken and defeated, James did something I never expected.

Instead of leaving me and starting over fresh with somebody new... he stayed.

The same man who had once hurt me proved that redemption was possible. In the years that followed, he began his own journey of healing and transformation, addressing the underlying causes of his abusive behavior. Through self-reflection, he became a changed man who sincerely apologized for the pain he had caused and worked tirelessly, promising to become the husband I had always deserved.

It was a long and challenging road that required tremendous strength and resilience. His journey had been filled with highs and lows as he battled the complexities of his own abusive childhood.

James fought valiantly to reclaim his sense of self and unearth the love and light buried beneath the rubble of his past. In doing so, he found the strength not only to heal himself but also to save me. I had always admired James for his strength and kindness, but it wasn't until my darkest days that I realized the extent of his love and power.

THE HEALING BEGINS

Due to years of abuse, my struggles with mental health began slowly, like discontented whispers that grew louder with each passing day.

Anxiety was a constant companion who whispered doubts and fears into my ears.

Depression soon followed, like a heavy cloak on my shoulders, making every step a struggle.

When I was diagnosed with PTSD, the darkness seemed to seep into my soul, enveloping me in a cloud of despair.

And when I entered a full state of psychosis, requiring admission into a psychiatric hospital, life as I knew it was over.

James was the one who first noticed the difference in me, the subtle changes in my behavior, and the light that was gradually dimming in my eyes. He approached me with gentleness and warmth, his eyes reflecting his heart's concern. He listened intently as I tried to describe the indescribable turmoil raging within me.

I found a ray of hope in his unwavering support. He encouraged me to seek professional assistance, emphasizing the importance of confronting these demons with guidance and therapy. James took the first step of finding and getting me into therapy. After many failed sessions with many different therapists, he finally found two amazing women, Dr. Kelly Horton and Dr. Marchita Masters, who would play an essential role in my healing process.

The road to recovery was extremely grueling. I had decades of abuse to unpack. I wanted to give up at times when the darkness threatened to overwhelm me. I grew tired of the numerous hospitalizations, the medications and the psychotic induced suicide attempts.

But James never left my side, he came to every therapy session, held me up through the most challenging times, and celebrated the small victories along the way.

To better understand my new reality, James enrolled himself in online classes and courses, spending countless hours learning about my mental health struggles and everyday challenges. He adapted his strategy to account for my triggers and needs. He became my advocate and ally in the battle against mental illness, rescuing me from the depths of my own mind.

PTSD induced flashbacks and hallucinations ravaged my mind day after day, night after night, leaving me breathless and paralyzed by fear. In those moments, James would hold me close, whispering words of comfort and love until the panic subsided. He realized the value of a gentle touch, a kind word, and a calm presence. During my darkest nights, he was the lighthouse guiding me back to safety.

Throughout the ups and downs of my recovery, James was patient and understanding. He reminded me that recovery was a marathon, not a sprint. He taught me that love can heal even the deepest wounds, and that compassion and understanding can bridge the gap between a broken heart and a healing heart.

Tears streamed down my face the day I realized how far I had come. It was a poignant moment of clarity, a realization that James' unwavering love and support had aided my progress significantly. His belief in me had bolstered my determination to overcome the darkness that threatened to consume me.

James not only saved our marriage, but also my life. His love had been a lifeline, a ray of hope when all seemed lost. He showed me that love has the ability to heal, uplift, and cast light into the darkest corners of our souls.

As I sit here today, reflecting on that turbulent period in my life, I am grateful for the healing that took place. James and I have come a long way together, supporting each other through highs and lows and finding solace in our love. We have both become authors, sharing our stories to inspire other women and men who have found themselves in similar situations.

Our wounds may never heal completely, but they have become scars, a reminder of the battles we fought and the strength we discovered within ourselves and each other.

I discovered that love, no matter how tarnished or broken, can heal and mend. Through the darkest times, love kept us going. It gave us the courage to confront our demons and eventually brought light into our lives.

REACHING OUT, REJECTION, AND RESILIENCE

I never thought I'd be the one to turn to "extended" family for help. But desperate times tend to blur the lines we draw around pride and necessity. Shortly after my discharge from the hospital, I found myself facing a maze of uncertainty, stumbling through a labyrinth of medical bills and a turbulent mental health journey. That's when I remembered a distant uncle, an uncle I hadn't seen in decades but who was the pastor of his own church, a man I thought I could turn to for guidance and support.

Visiting him at his church felt surreal. The years had etched their marks on our faces, but as we exchanged pleasantries, there was an air of familiarity that eased the initial tension.

My husband stood by my side as we sat across from his desk, ready to unravel the struggles I was facing.

The warmth in his initial greeting quickly chilled as I explained my situation. The mention of hospitalizations and mental illness seemed to cast an uncomfortable shadow over his features. His inquiries steered toward religion and faith, as if my struggles could simply be resolved by rekindling a connection to something I had distanced myself from over time.

I attempted to convey my beliefs in God along with a spirituality that didn't align neatly with a specific religious label. But to him, my lack of regular church attendance and my unconventional relationship with religion overshadowed any practical discussion about possible assistance or resources.

My uncle spoke of the devil's presence in my life, suggesting prayer and a revival of religious faith as the panacea to my predicament. We bowed our heads, his words of prayer hanging heavy in the air, and then abruptly, he escorted us out of his office, citing an urgent meeting.

His secretary, a witness to our brief encounter, promised to pass along our phone numbers, but it was an empty reassurance. Days turned into weeks, and weeks into months, with our calls met by silence. James tried leaving messages on my behalf, hoping for a change in the tide, but the waves of indifference crashed upon our efforts.

The disappointment settled like a heavy cloak over my shoulders. The realization that I was on my own, yet again, slowly crept in. It was a sharp reminder that sometimes, family ties can't bridge the gap between differing beliefs and perspectives. The door I thought would open to support and aid was now firmly shut, leaving me standing in a cold abandonment.

I never sought his help again, nor did I try to breach the wall of silence that encased his world. The echoes of unanswered calls and unreturned messages became a poignant reminder of my need for self-reliance. I forged ahead, navigating the maze of my troubles without the expected familial buoyancy.

Even now, many years later, that chapter remains closed. The unanswered calls have become a distant memory, a testament to the resilience and independence that adversity can nurture. The absence of his support, though disappointing, became a catalyst for self-discovery. It reinforced my resilience, teaching me that I was the sturdiest pillar I could lean on. I learned to trust my own strength, to weave through the challenges that life presented, without expecting a lifeline from those I had once considered family.

FAMILY GHOSTING

Reflecting on that meeting with my distant uncle made me reconsider the dynamics in my family; I couldn't help but notice this perplexing pattern that weaves through generations, almost like an unspoken script passed down through the years. It's a tale of favoritism, where the kids deemed "less favored" by their parents find themselves echoing that same marginalization within the larger family circle.

I wish I could say it's a rarity, a one-off occurrence, but it's far too common. The heartbreaking part? It's not just confined to the parental domain; it seeps into the aunts, uncles, and cousins, cascading like a domino effect of indifference.

This realization hit me like a freight train—watching Ms. Lady treat me as insignificant was tough enough, but witnessing the echo of that behavior in the extended family was a different kind of pain. It's like wearing an invisible coat of unimportance, and no matter how hard you try to shrug it off, it lingers, a constant shadow casting its gloom over family gatherings and interactions.

Ms. Lady didn't mince words about it. She made it known, not just within the four walls of our home but to anyone willing to lend an ear. The sting of her indifference was sharp, a relentless reminder that I wasn't quite the apple of her eye. But what cuts even deeper is seeing echoes of that sentiment mirrored in other family members.

It's a peculiar phenomenon—I've interacted with relatives who barely acknowledge my existence, as if my presence was inconsequential. The hurtful part is not just the lack of engagement; it's the subtle cues, the dismissive glances, the way conversations effortlessly skirt around me, leaving me stranded in a sea of overlooked emotions.

The sting of feeling insignificant within your own family is a lacerating pain. You'd think that within the "tight-knit fabric of family," you'd always feel valued and seen. But sometimes, the reality is a stark contrast. You attend family gatherings and engage in conversations, yet you're a ghost, a fleeting shadow. Your words dissipate into the air, your presence fades into the background, and your significance dwindles into nothingness.

It's a pain that lingers beyond the immediate moment, seeping into every aspect of life. It influences how you perceive yourself, shaping your confidence and affecting how you navigate relationships beyond the familial realm.

And what baffles me most is the unabashed nature of it all. It's as if those replicating these behaviors had adopted this script without a second thought, perpetuating a cycle they might not even be aware of. Maybe it all stems from the ease with which these patterns are accepted, the lack of critical introspection, or perhaps it's just easier to maintain the status quo than challenge ingrained family dynamics.

But here's the truth—it shouldn't be this way. Children should never bear the burden of parental favoritism, and certainly not the ripple effect of it within the broader family spectrum. The wounds from parental neglect are already deep, and adding the collective indifference of extended family members creates scars that take a lifetime to heal.

I've often pondered on why this happens—is it an unconscious replication of what they've witnessed in their own upbringing or a lack of empathy towards the intricate emotional landscape of a child's world? Perhaps it's a blend of both, intertwined with societal norms and an unspoken hierarchy that deems some worthy of attention and others not.

But understanding the 'why' doesn't alleviate the pain. It's an ache that lingers, a narrative I wish to rewrite. And while I navigate through these familial waters, I find solace in the fact that awareness breeds change. Acknowledging this silent struggle might be the first step towards breaking this unforgiving cycle, paving the way for a more inclusive, compassionate family.

It took me almost 50 years to realize my insignificance isn't a truth; it's a perception, a distortion that can be shattered. I realized that the acknowledgment or validation of others didn't define my worth. My voice held weight and my presence mattered, regardless of whether it was acknowledged.

MY COUSINS

A rollercoaster of emotions and experiences shaped the person I am today. Looking back, the echoes of those years often stir a mix of nostalgia, regret, and a profound realization of how our perceptions change with time.

One of the most poignant memories etched in my mind is the bittersweet tale of familial bonds... or better said, the lack thereof. As a child, I grappled with the inexplicable disparity in Ms. Lady's affection. It was a peculiar phenomenon that left an indelible mark on my heart from a young age.

I watched silently as she lavished her love and attention on my cousins. A painful spectacle, one that stung deeper with each passing year. I couldn't fathom why her love flowed effortlessly toward them while I was engulfed in a sea of neglect, disdain and outright abuse. Trying to understand her behavior was like those reading assignments that made my head spin, but it was a realization that burrowed its way into my heart, breeding a bitterness that I unknowingly directed towards my cousins.

In the recesses of my heart, bitterness found a place to call home. It wasn't something I welcomed, but it seemed to be the only emotion I could fully understand at the time. It was easier to direct that bitterness toward my cousins rather than understand the deeper-rooted issues festering within me.

In my innocence, I failed to realize that they were mere recipients of affection, innocent souls embraced by the warmth of Ms. Lady's love. How could I fault them for accepting something so pure and fundamental? All they knew was the tenderness she offered, a love they rightfully deserved.

As I journeyed through life, carrying the weight of misunderstood emotions, I began to understand the complexity of human relationships. My resentment towards my cousins was a misplaced projection of my hurt. I know now that they were not to blame for the love they received. They were innocent bystanders in a narrative written by circumstances beyond their control.

To my cousins,

I apologize for the distance I inadvertently created. I apologize for my actions, fueled by unresolved childhood wounds if they have caused you pain. I never meant to push you away or sow seeds of discord between us.

It took time for me to understand that Ms. Lady's actions weren't a reflection of my worth. Her love, or the lack thereof, was a complex tapestry woven from her own experiences and insecurities. Understanding this didn't magically heal the wounds, but it softened the edges of my bitterness.

Your visible absence in my life has marked the years spent apart. I've missed the laughter, the shared moments, and the camaraderie we once had. There's a yearning to bridge the chasm I allowed to grow between us, to reclaim what was lost in the turbulent haze of the past.

I long for a future where we can reconcile and forge new memories together. The prospect of reconnecting with you, of rediscovering the bonds we once shared, fills me with hope and a sense of anticipation for what lies ahead.

In life, the threads of our relationships may fray and tangle, but with time and understanding, there's always a chance to weave them back together, creating a stronger and more resilient bond than before.

BECOMING A FOSTER PARENT

As I reflect through the chapters of my life, I can't help but see the intricate patterns woven into my existence. It's as though the moments, the choices, and the challenges all came together like patches on a quilt; each square, each moment, part of a larger design, one that took shape as I navigated through the threads of my past.

Growing older has a way of stirring things up within you. It brings those forgotten memories back to life, like old photographs fading in an attic. I found myself reflecting on my difficult childhood, the missing pieces, and the love that was absent. It fueled a fire in me, a need to give back to those who, like me, had felt the sting of neglect and abuse.

So, I made a decision, one that wasn't just about changing lives but about bringing purpose to my own existence. I wanted to be there for children who needed safety and warmth. I wanted to provide children with the unwavering affection that I, unfortunately, missed out on. When I shared my desire to become a foster parent with my husband, his initial reaction was not favorable, but eventually, his hesitation melted away when he saw the passion burning in my eyes.

My dyslexia posed its challenges, but it never became an insurmountable obstacle. I enrolled in an evening training program, balancing the demands of a full-time job during the day. James stood by my side, a pillar of support attending every class, absorbing every bit of information from the literature that seemed to dance and sway beyond my comprehension. His commitment was my lifeline, guiding me through the maze of reading requirements and preparations.

Becoming a licensed foster parent was laborious; filled with extensive background checks, CPR and first aid training, endless home inspections, and long, exhaustive parenting classes. But the day I received my foster care license, it felt like I was holding the key to a whole new world of possibilities. It was like unlocking a treasure of boundless opportunities.

I chose to focus on the youngest children, newborns to two-year-olds; it felt like my calling. When I held that first little girl, just removed from a home of neglect, it felt like I was cradling hope in my arms. As the months progressed, the social worker was touched by the love and dedication I showered the child with. She revealed a pressing need for foster parents for this age range, especially those willing to care for children with special needs.

So, my husband and I returned to the classroom, to become a Licensed Ambulatory Foster Care Home. It was a commitment unlike any other, being on call 24 hours a day, 7 days a week. I remember one 2 a.m. call, a newborn whose life was already a tangle of complications due to a mother's methamphetamine addiction. We drove to that hospital in Kingsburg, California, red-eyed and tired but brimming with excitement and determination.

That little bundle of joy became our world for close to a year, however, witnessing her battle through withdrawal was heartbreaking. She cried and screamed for hours on end, day and night, as her tiny body hosted a battleground against the remnants of her mother's choices. It was an arduous journey, but the love we poured into her was relentless and unwavering.

For over a decade, my cell phone became a lifeline to children in desperate need. Neglect, abuse, drug addiction—each brought their own unique set of trials. There were triumphs and moments of sheer delight as these little hearts bloomed under the nurturing shelter of my love, safety, and care.

Yet, there were also the heartaches—the kind that embroider themselves into the very fabric of your soul. I was caring for a newborn whose mother tested positive for HIV, and despite the love and support we showered the baby with... God called the infant home.

The path of a foster parent is a bittersweet odyssey. The scars of my own past found their purpose by tending to the wounds of these innocent souls. Each child that crossed my threshold became a story, a vibrant patch in the quilt of my life. Each patch was woven with threads of hope and an unrelenting desire to illuminate their world with love, kindness, and safety.

MY TIME AS
A DAYCARE OWNER

Becoming a foster parent wasn't something I stumbled upon in a grand epiphany. It was a gradual realization that unfolded before my eyes as I reflected on my childhood. The joy of fulfilling the needs of other children, witnessing their growth, and helping them heal brought immeasurable satisfaction.

But then came a moment when the line between fostering and starting a daycare blurred. The social workers started asking if I offered daycare services. It was a seed of an idea I had yet to consider: Could I transition from fostering to daycare and still feel the same sense of purpose?

My husband saw the opportunity for growth. He believed in my ability to expand my services, but I grappled with the dilemma of choosing between the two—being a foster parent or a daycare provider. How could I give up one for the other when both touched my heart in such different ways?

Amid my conflict, fate seemed to intervene. I stumbled upon information about obtaining dual licensing for foster care and daycare. I was beyond excited! It was as if the universe was urging me to embrace this new path that combined my passions.

The journey began with enthusiasm, and soon, our home was transformed into a daycare facility. It was a realm where play and learning intertwined seamlessly. However, I wanted to make our services more than just a daycare. I had a desire to cater to a specific need in our community—single mothers without transportation.

That's when the idea of offering free transportation for these mothers surfaced. I wanted to transport their children to and from the daycare. My husband shared my vision, and together, we delved into research, exploring ways to make transportation accessible for these families. We needed a vehicle to accommodate multiple children, ensuring safe and reliable transportation.

We headed to our local Nissan dealership; our hearts filled with the anticipation of making a difference. I spotted the perfect fit as we walked through rows of cars—a seven-passenger Nissan Armada. It was more than a vehicle; it was about breaking down barriers, removing obstacles, and enabling these mothers to access childcare without worrying about getting their children there. It was going to make their lives a little easier and their burdens a little lighter.

Driving that Armada off the dealership lot felt like embarking on a journey beyond just the roads. It was a journey toward empowerment and support for these mothers who were striving to create a better life for their families.

The first day I offered the transportation service was filled with a mix of excitement and nervousness. As the Armada pulled up, the smiles on the faces of the mothers waiting outside their apartments said more than words ever could. It was a moment of relief, gratitude, and knowing they could rely on me to help them in this small but significant way.

With this addition, my daycare became a haven for neglected children and a lifeline for single mothers striving to provide for their families. Word spread, and soon, I found myself with a waiting list—a testament to the impact I was making in my community.

With every trip, the Armada became more than a vehicle. It became a symbol of hope, a bridge connecting families to the care their children deserved. And for me, it was a reminder of the power of simple ideas and the support of a loving partner.

I found solace in this dual role. The daycare allowed me to extend care beyond the foster system, touching the lives of struggling mothers. And yet, fostering remained an integral part of our purpose. Both filled my days with meaning and fulfillment.

Through this journey, I realized that our purpose in life isn't confined to a single path. Sometimes, it's about blending our passions, adapting, and creating something that encompasses all we hold dear. Once again, I had found my niche— a space where neglected children found love, single mothers found support, and I found my calling.

COLLEGE

Education always felt like a game of catch-up for me. Dyslexia, that tricky condition, had been my unwanted sidekick since childhood. Words on pages danced around, making textbooks feel like decoding a foreign language. Kids can be tough, and my classmates were no exception. Their teasing and whispers left stains on my confidence, like shadows that never entirely disappeared. Even some family members chimed in, adding their own harsh notes to my struggles.

Then came that low blow from my daughter's father, Lee; his words felt like a stab to the heart, carving deeper insecurities into my soul. He warned our rebellious daughter, "If you don't get your shit together, you are going to end up worthless, just like your mother," echoing my own fears and haunting my aspirations. Once again, casting those shadows over me.

Psychosis barged into my life uninvited, unknowingly setting its roots in my mind around 2012. The medications prescribed felt like a double-edged sword, blurring my reality while adding 40 pounds of weight to my body. So, I took matters into my own hands, delving into Ayurveda and holistic approaches and transforming my lifestyle and diet. By 2014, I stood medication-free, my head above water for a while.

In 2018, I dared to step onto the college path, my lifelong dream dangling before me. But reality hit harder than expected. That first semester became a battleground with jealous female professors, their envy and prejudice scarring my academic pursuit. The second semester proved life altering. An older Caucasian male professor, blinded by his sexual thirst, dragged me into a nightmarish spiral.

Fighting off his sexual advances became a trigger, igniting my PTSD and summoning my pain back to the surface.

Initially, I didn't confide in my husband about the professor's sexual harassment, fearing the uncontrollable beast he would become in my defense. Despite the torment eating away at my sanity, I vowed to forge ahead. But the stress was too heavy for my fragile mind. Unresolved childhood wounds reopened Pandora's box of buried trauma.

I lost my grip on reality. The lines blurred, and I slipped into the treacherous terrain of psychosis. Looking back, I harbor no regrets about seizing control of my health or stepping onto the college grounds. My husband walked through the flames of hell with me detailing our journey in his autobiography, "In Love with My 5 Wives: A Broken Man's Journey on How to Love His Broken Wife." His love and dedication pulled me back from the edge of that abyss.

In the haze of those memories, what remains *Crystal* clear is the strength forged in those battles. My scars, although invisible to most, are badges of survival. They etch a story of resilience in my soul.

A newfound clarity emerges as I trace back the steps through that tumultuous period. The battle that took place in my mind might lack vivid details, but the emotions stand tall, reminding me of my strength and the unwavering support that guided me through the storm.

BECOMING AN AUTHOR

Never in a million years did I think I'd find myself here, a published author. Books have always been my sanctuary, my escape into worlds far beyond my own. But the irony of it all! Reading, for me, was like navigating a maze blindfolded.

Dyslexia danced through the words on the page, turning letters into a kaleidoscope of confusion. The thought of writing my own book? It seemed like a fantasy woven from threads of impossibility.

Life, however, can take the most unexpected path. My journey to becoming an author was a winding road riddled with obstacles that seemed impossible. But within those challenges lay the seeds of my inspiration.

Mental illness became an uninvited guest, changing the trajectory of my life and the dream of physically caring for children was torn from my grasp. Yet, during this tumultuous period, amidst the chaos of a bout with psychosis, a spark ignited within me.

Charlie and The Magic Tree emerged during one of those inexplicable, psychotic moments. In the depths of my mind, amidst the kaleidoscope of thoughts, the concept blossomed like a flower in the desert. It was as if the universe had whispered its secrets to me. I felt compelled to share this magical tale, a story that transcended the boundaries of my reality.

It was a daunting revelation. How could I, with my struggles in reading and writing, weave a story worth telling? And then, there was him – my husband. I poured out the fragments of my imagination to him, the vivid imagery that danced in my mind's eye. We stitched the pieces together, creating a narrative that seemed to breathe with life.

Crafting the story of Charlie and her enchanting tree became our shared endeavor. Each word was a triumph over the barriers that sought to confine me. And when the tale felt complete, my husband, already a successful self-published author, brought my creation to life.

The moment my book graced the digital shelves of Amazon felt surreal. In less than two days, Charlie and The Magic Tree ascended to the top as the #1 new release in the category of "Children's Forest & Tree Books." It was a moment of validation, a testament that dreams, no matter how improbable, could sprout wings and soar.

But the journey didn't end there. Inspiration struck once more, this time in the form of extending Charlie's world. A coloring book and activity workbooks bloomed from the fertile soil of my imagination. It was my way of reaching out and touching the lives of countless children, offering them not just a story but an interactive journey into literacy and creativity.

Creating these companion pieces felt like nurturing a garden, each page a new bud waiting to bloom. The joy of knowing that these books might ignite a passion for reading and writing in young hearts, that they might ease the struggles of those, like me, facing the daunting challenge of dyslexia – was a purpose I never knew I'd find.

Caring for children had taken on a new guise. My love for them now stretched far beyond the confines of physical presence. Through the magic of words, illustrations, and activities, I found a way to weave a tapestry that could combat illiteracy and make learning to read and write a little less daunting.

The journey from a woman battling her own mind to becoming a beacon of imagination for children was as miraculous as the story of Charlie and her magical tree. It was proof that within the depths of our struggles lies the potential to create something beautiful, something that transcends the barriers we perceive as impossible.

As I sit here, I'm filled with a warmth that surpasses the joy of seeing my book soar. It's the satisfaction of knowing that Charlie and The Magic Tree might light a spark in a child's heart, guiding them through the beautiful world of words. And in that possibility, my journey finds its ultimate fulfillment.

My mother only had me for the check ...and it finally paid off.

MY BEAUTIFUL SISTERS DR. KELLY HORTON & DR. MARCHITA MASTERS

As I reflect on my journey to healing and recovery, I can't help but be grateful for the extraordinary influence Dr. Kelly Horton and Dr. Marchita Masters have had on my life. These beautiful African-American women played pivotal roles in guiding me through the maze of my past and leading me to a future of hope and strength.

Dr. Kelly Horton became a pillar of comfort in my life, filling a void I didn't even realize existed—a big sister figure I never had. Her warm, nurturing demeanor put me at ease from the start of our therapeutic relationship. Dr. Horton had a natural talent for making me feel heard, understood, and valued. She embraced me in a compassionate and understanding manner, much like an older sister would. She knew exactly what I needed, sometimes even before I did.

Dr. Horton's unwavering honesty and directness were two of her most distinguishing characteristics. She was never afraid to confront me, to point out my fears and doubts, and to encourage me to face them head-on. It was like having a mentor who was genuinely concerned about my growth and development. Dr.

Horton's "keep it real" approach to life's challenges gave me the perspective I needed to navigate the complexities of my past traumas and their aftereffects. Her advice was a ray of light in my darkest hours, providing the reassurance I needed to keep going.

Our sessions were about more than just dealing with my problems; they were about embracing life's journey with all its complexities. Dr. Horton frequently shared

stories from her own life, displaying both vulnerability and strength. Through her, I learned that facing challenges and learning from them is essential to personal development.

Due to changes in insurance benefits, our time soon came to an end, and it was a difficult day for me to say goodbye. I was aware that I was losing a significant influence in my life. Dr. Horton has given me the tools and mindset to face the world with newfound strength, and I will be eternally grateful for her, and our time spent together.

Dr. Marchita Masters played a different but equally important role in my healing journey. She was the motherly figure I had never had, providing me with the guidance, wisdom, and unconditional love I had craved throughout my turbulent childhood. Dr. Masters approached our sessions with a nurturing embrace, allowing me to share my deepest fears and pains in a safe, nonjudgmental environment.

Dr. Masters encouraged me to explore my emotions, assisting me in understanding and accepting them as an essential part of my healing process. She gently reassured me, allowing me to heal at my own pace and offered guidance like a mother guiding her child. Her wisdom and compassion helped me rebuild my faith in myself and the possibility of a better future.

She used a combination of evidence-based practices and her own extensive experience to tailor a personalized approach to my healing throughout our sessions. She was skilled at navigating the complexities of my past traumas and current struggles by combining psychological theories, therapeutic techniques, and her keen intuition. Every session brought me closer to understanding myself and finding the strength to overcome my pain.

Dr. Masters's expertise in trauma therapy was invaluable in my healing process. She effectively guided me through trauma-focused cognitive-behavioral techniques, giving me the tools and strategies I needed to process and overcome my past wounds. Her ability to explain complex concepts in simple terms, combined with her unwavering patience, enabled me to grasp and effectively apply these techniques.

Beyond her academic achievements, Dr. Masters was distinguished by her genuine concern and compassion. She was more than just a psychologist; she became a confidante. Her ability to empathize, truly listen, and understand my pain demonstrated her commitment as a healer and mentor.

My sessions with Dr. Masters have provided me with a consistent and loving source of support over the years. She has been a constant presence in my life, guiding me through the ups and downs of healing. Her continuing faith in my abilities has served as a source of motivation and a reminder that I am deserving of love and happiness.

I am eternally grateful for Dr. Horton's and Dr. Masters' dynamic influences in my life. Each brought their own perspective, filling gaps and nurturing me in ways critical to my growth and recovery. Thanks to their guidance and unwavering support, I've emerged more robust, more resilient, and better equipped to face life's challenges. Their influence continues to reverberate in my life, reminding me daily of my inner strength and the love that surrounds me.

To My Sisters Around the World

As I sit here, I find myself enveloped in a world of emotions, a tapestry woven from the threads of my past and the vibrant hues of my present. My fingers trace the scars, both visible and hidden, the remnants of a life once marred by abuse, neglect, and the crushing weight of shattered dreams. Yet, at this moment, I stand tall, a testament to the resilience that beats within the heart of every woman who has felt the sting of adversity.

The echoes of my journey reverberate through the corridors of time, resonating with the pain of countless nights spent shrouded in fear, my bruises serving as a cruel testament to the darkness that clouded my existence. I was a canvas painted with the hues of torment, a portrait of a woman on the brink of surrender. But within the depths of my despair flickered a tiny flame of defiance, a spark that refused to be snuffed out.

I remember the day I dared to step away from the shadows, the trembling uncertainty as I took those tentative steps toward a new dawn. It was a journey riddled with obstacles, self-doubt, and hesitance. But with each faltering step, I reclaimed a piece of my shattered spirit. The scars became not badges of shame but marks of survival—a testament to the strength that lay dormant within me.

The path toward love was fraught with trepidation, for the wounds of the past cast long shadows on the landscape of my heart. Yet, love found me in the most unexpected of moments, not as a savior to rescue me, but as a companion to walk alongside me on this tumultuous journey.

Through the gentle touch of understanding, I learned to embrace my worth and cherish the resilience that had carried me through the storm.

Becoming an author was my liberation— an anthem of defiance against the silence imposed upon me. With each word etched upon the pages, I unraveled the tangled knots of my soul, breathing life into stories that danced between fiction and the raw tapestry of my reality. I became the architect of my narrative, wielding my words as a weapon against the ghosts of my past. Through the power of storytelling, I found solace, healing, and the freedom to articulate the unspoken truths that resonated with the hearts of many.

To my sisters who walk a path similar to mine, hear me now: you are not defined by the shackles of your past. Your scars are not the sum of your story but reminders of the battles you've fought and the strength that courses through your veins. In the depths of your struggle lies an unyielding courage—a flame waiting to be kindled, waiting to ignite a symphony of resilience.

I love you—not with mere words, but with a love borne from shared struggles, a love that transcends the barriers of time and circumstance. You are not alone. Your journey, though unique, is a thread woven into the vast tapestry of womanhood—a testament to the resilience and unyielding strength that resides within.

Never relinquish the reins that guide your destiny. Hold onto the pen that scripts your life with a steadfast determination. Let your story be an anthem of triumph, a narrative that sings of resilience, courage, and the unwavering belief in the power you hold to reshape your reality.

Rise and embrace the canvas of your life. Paint it with strokes of courage, resilience, and unbridled hope. Your journey is proof of the infinite possibilities that await those who refuse to be defined by their past.

With a love that knows no bounds, with a hope that springs eternal, and with an unwavering belief in your indomitable spirit,

Your Sister,

Crystal Bass

This book grabbed me with its captivating storytelling which unabashedly lays bare the author's mind-bending journey from abused child to abused woman. It covers her decent into severe mental illness and her desperate attempts to claw her way back. This book also brutally illustrates a mother's callous disregard for her own child's needs and feelings while refusing to protect her from her abusers.

The author, Crystal Bass, has a way of painting a picture of her life so it can be clearly seen, but most would never want to see, much less experience what she experienced. Crystal was an innocent little girl who only wanted her mother's love. She stated the title of this book, "My Mother Only Had Me for the Check," is a true statement and was reminded of this painful reality day after day, week after week and year after year.

I believe when children are abused, it would be wonderful if they were rewarded with a trouble-free adulthood to compensate but that's not usually the way it works out. Unfortunately, when a child is abused (emotionally, physically, sexually, and/or verbally), it is incredibly traumatic and causes deep emotional injuries that can last a lifetime.

Abuse leaves an indelible mark on the psyche often leading to low self-esteem, a distorted view of oneself and the world, dysfunctional communication patterns, chaotic relationships, and a range of mental health issues from depression and anxiety to PTSD and psychosis. Growing up in an abusive, chaotic household puts a child on a trajectory that almost guarantees more of the same in the future, and sadly but not surprisingly, this is Crystal's story.

Crystal went from an abused child who struggled to read, to an abused woman who struggled to read. Even with those major traumas, she became a foster mother and entrepreneur. She loved her foster babies and day care kids. She poured love into the tiniest and most vulnerable among us. She longed for this sort of love when she was young, and it was almost like she was loving her "inner child" by loving them.

Like so many others, Crystal began to suffer from mental illness. Her time as a foster parent and daycare owner had come to an end; it was just her and her formerly abusive husband, James. He sprang into action obtaining all sorts of treatment for her, including starting telehealth therapy with me. Over time and with lots of love from James and treatment from various providers, she began to show signs of improvement and eventually recovered. She now writes about her experiences to help others understand mental illness and to shine a light on the horrific reality of child abuse and domestic violence. Crystal also has a series of children's books and workbooks called "Charlie and the Magic Tree" where she helps African-American children feel pride in their skin color and natural hair while learning to read and write.

Of course, she'd want to help others in areas where she herself struggled. Her journey through childhood abuse, domestic violence, entrepreneurship, mental illness and eventually becoming a published author is simply astonishing.

I am very proud to have assisted Crystal on her journey. She is a very special person. Her past was bleak, but she found a way to continue to heal. Maya Angelou said "Leaving behind nights of terror and fear, I rise. Into a daybreak that's wondrously clear, I rise." Crystal rose and continues to rise high, smashing every obstacle and always remembering to reach back to help others. This is who she is, a wonderful human being, an inspiration, and not just a kid who was created for a check.

Dr. Marchita Masters

MasterOurMentalHealth.com

Pediatric, Adult and Family Psychologist

Resources

- National Suicide and Crisis Lifeline (www.988lifeline. org or call 988)

- National Alliance on Mental Illness (www.nami.org)

- Substance Abuse and Mental Health Services Administration (www.samhsa.gov)

- National Institute on Alcohol Abuse and Alcoholism (www.niaaa.nih.gov)

- Childhelp National Child Abuse Hotline (www. childhelphotline.org)

- Find a therapist in your area (www.psychologytoday. com)